In Search of Growth

OTHER TITLES FROM
LIVING CHURCH BOOKS

❊ ❊ ❊

Vol. 1: *God Wills Fellowship*, edited by
Christopher Wells and Jeremy Worthen

Vol. 2: *When Churches in Communion Disagree*,
edited by Robert Heaney, Christopher Wells &
Pierre Whalon

Vol 3. *Pastoral Ministrations of the Priest*,
compiled, arranged, and edited
by Matthew S.C. Olver

In Search of Growth

THE EDITORS OF THE LIVING CHURCH

LIVING CHURCH BOOKS

Contents

PART II:
Profiles

PART III:
Practical Wisdom

INTRO

Introduction

Mark Michael

I planted, Apollos watered,
but God gave the growth.

—I Corinthians 3:6

God gives the growth. The earth's perennial yet unpredictable fertility manifests his generosity, each plant and animal containing within it the means to give life to another. His word descends to us in power, and lives are changed as surely as seeds sprout and leaves unfurl. "It shall accomplish that which I purpose, and prosper in the thing for which I sent it," he assures us (Isa. 55:11). He is the great Sower, Jesus tells us, who sends his laborers to the world's far corners to plant and water, and share the joy of the harvest.

The apostolic church was marked by growth. Revealed by the Holy Spirit at Pentecost amid a crowd "from every nation under heaven," we track its growing membership by the numbers carefully recorded in the Book of Acts. Propelled from Jerusalem by persecution, we see the Spirit's work as it reaches across cultural barriers, "becoming all things to all men'" through bold and winsome preaching of our crucified and risen Lord. The Spirit heals the sick, consoles the broken, and makes great saints of sinners like us.

No subsequent age has ever quite recaptured the apostolic Church's dynamism and zeal, but the Spirit still moves and works among us. God gives growth, sometimes in unexpected ways. Even amid the multi-generational decline faced by the Episcopal Church and most of Anglicanism in the West, there are still thriving churches, and strategies that bear fruit in sharing the gospel with a world that still longs to know and love God, even when it hardly knows his name.

Over the last several years, from our distinctive "watch tower," *The Living Church* has been spotting these signs of growth within the Episcopal Church. In this volume, we have gathered together our best analysis of the current challenges and opportunities for sharing the good news. We profile churches in many different contexts that are trying new things and finding an eager response. We also include essays from *Covenant* contributors about practices shared by many growing churches.

We hope to encourage church leaders, to spark new ideas, to strengthen good things God has already begun. We pray for continued growth and renewal in this part of his Church.

Mark A. Michael
Feast of the Visitation, 2024

PART I

On Church Decline & Growth

❄ ❄ ❄

ONE

Learning from England: Lessons in Church Growth

Jordan Hylden

What makes a church grow? If the recent polling by Gallup[1] is any indication, there are many church leaders asking that question these days who are not too sure of the answer. Since I was a teenager in youth group back in the late 1990s, church membership has dropped alarmingly: down from 70% to 47% today. That is a lot of decline in just twenty years. Savvier writers than I have debated what's behind it — highly publicized sex abuse scandals, historic shifts away from traditional Christian teaching on marriage and sexuality, and political polarization all surely have something to do with it. But whatever it is, church leaders today need to be very aware that complacency will not do. Those of us charged with leadership need to be active learners and prayerful penitents, seeking out what God is doing to renew his Church

---

1   https://news.gallup.com/poll/341963/church-membership-falls-below-majori-ty-first-time.aspx

and humbly open to what God may also be doing to chasten and judge.

There are, of course, shelves full of books on church growth and leadership going back decades. I try to make it a habit to learn from these books, but some of them by now are a bit dated, and some could stand to be a bit more theologically and sacramentally grounded. That's why I recently read two books that seek to learn from church growth in England, where the secularizing trends that have picked up steam in the U.S. already happened decades ago, and where the Church of England gives myriad examples that are readily translatable to the sacramental worship of the Episcopal Church. If it's growing in the good old C of E, it's probably something we Episcopalians can learn from. Even better, the two books — *Learning from London* by Jason Fout, and *Northern Lights* by Jason Byassee — were written by scholar-pastors, trained as theologians and with a heart for the local church. I highly recommend both. What then can we learn from the church in Old Blighty?

DO THE BASICS WELL.

Byassee begins his book with a few observations that should surprise no one: "It seems to me the keys for growth are several: a clear and compelling mission, able and energetic leadership (preferably in place for a long period of time), a welcoming congregation engaged in mission, attention paid to discipleship and growth."

There are many ways to do all of that, and his book, focused on church growth in the very secular region of northern England, tells the story of a wide variety of growing churches: conservative and contemporary evangelical, ancient cathedrals with high church traditional worship, and socially progressive churches heavily involved in social justice work. Both Byassee and Fout make clear that growth is not the exclusive preserve of one style of churchmanship over another. In that sense, there is no magic bullet: it's just not true that if you add screens and guitars, or choral Evensong for that matter, they will come!

It does however seem to be true that a church that's clear and intentional about its mission does better than one that's fuzzy about what it believes or has a hard time focusing its collective efforts. The Diocese of London, Fout writes, expects its parishes to come up with outward-focused Mission Action Plans and to report back their self-assessment on how they're doing every year.

It also seems clear that growing churches tend to be ones with long-serving rectors or vicars. A constant churn of leadership puts the brakes on long-term growth, for obvious reasons. This isn't a new lesson for us, of course, but it does help in the C of E that clergy salaries are standardized churchwide: there's no leaving to seek better pay elsewhere, so perhaps less incentive to go. There are definite advantages to this arrangement, but it is unlikely that TEC will adopt it anytime soon. So long as we don't, any church will need to think about whether their clergy and staff are compensated in such a way that it's easy for their families to stick around, instead of easy for them to feel pressured to look elsewhere.

Being genuinely welcoming is easier said than done. Yes, we say on the sign that "*The Episcopal Church Welcomes You*", but do we really? Fout makes the point that in many Episcopal congregations there are more graduate degrees than the general population has college degrees; for all of our talk about diversity, we tend to be a highly-educated, affluent bunch. As an established church, the C of E still has the sense that it's meant to be the church for everyone. Where it's growing, it's often because it's doing a good job at reaching out to average everyday people, not simply the highly educated few.

As our own Bishop Scott Benhase has recently noted, the bread-and-butter of church growth is about relationships: shaking the hands of newcomers, writing personal notes, telling people your "elevator speech" about why you love your church and inviting them to come, and so on. Part of Holy Trinity Brompton's explosive growth, Fout notes, came from a spiritual awakening that led them to grow in openness toward newcomers, really welcoming the stranger with warmth and relational vulnerability. We Episcopalians have, I'm afraid, too often earned our "frozen chosen" tagline, perhaps fearing invading someone else's privacy or being pushy about our faith.

Attention paid to discipleship, surely, is critical: church must be a place where we're invited and enabled to grow in faith, in prayer, in holiness, in servant love. It's intriguing that the Alpha Course, which has been behind so much growth in England and worldwide, began its life as a course at Holy Trinity Brompton to teach the basics of the faith to new members.

The list of "basics" could be extended: communications, facilities, web presence, and the like. But if a church has long-serving dedicated leadership, a clear and compelling mission, and is a warm, welcoming community, it's got a lot going for it.

CENTER ON THE GOSPEL OF THE RISEN AND LIVING CHRIST.

On theological grounds, of course, this is actually more "basic" than anything in the previous category. The growing churches surveyed by

Fout and Byassee, though they come in all shapes and sizes, are connected by a clear sense that the beating heart of their life and mission is the living God, the gospel of grace, Christ's atoning sacrifice for our sins, the new life and transformation given to us in the power of the Holy Spirit.

The growing churches they look at tend to be places of prayer. They pray expecting that God heals diseases, changes lives, and transforms hearts. They seek God's will, in full expectation that God will show up and lead his church. They preach Christ crucified and risen. They tell people about the good news of salvation in Jesus as if their lives depended on it. They are places where people are not afraid to speak openly, from the heart, about what Jesus has done in their lives, and not afraid to share Jesus with others.

Sam Wells writes in his foreword that *Northern Lights* is actually "a book about the Holy Spirit. Not a Spirit who has self-isolated into tongues and healings, but one who constantly, relentlessly, astonishingly makes the risen Christ present where all seemed lost, forlorn, forsaken." The same could be said of Fout's book, which attempts to describe why the Diocese of London has experienced remarkable growth in the very same period that almost all Anglican dioceses in the West have experienced decline. A great part of the story, Fout writes, is simply "openness to God," and an expectation that God is alive and acting through his Church right now. The churches Byassee and Fout write about tend not to have grown through increased professionalism or this or that program or technique. Instead, they've grown as they've listened intently and prayed fervently for God's leading and sought to follow where the Lord led.

In the follow-up to his post about relationships, Bishop Benhase makes a similar point, making clear that as basic as everything he said about relational ministry is, even more fundamental is the gospel of Jesus Christ. "The most critical point," Benhase writes, is a ministry focused "on God's grace imputed to sinners by Christ's cross." During his years recruiting in seminaries, Benhase relates how he made a practice of pretending to be an average Joe asking seminarians why he should join their church. Far too often, he writes, all they could come up with was something about great community, the music program, or active outreach — all of which he'd respond to by saying he didn't need church for that. "I waited patiently," Benhase writes, "for some mention of how their church could meet my greatest need, namely, to be reconciled with God through Jesus by his cross. Never came."

Perhaps the greatest thing we Episcopalians can learn from England is what many of the English learned years ago: when all of the other reasons people used to have to go to church fall away, the only good reason left is Jesus, his cross and our salvation. As it turns out, that is the only reason we've ever needed.

CHURCHES THAT INTEND TO GROW TEND TO GROW.

At the beginning of his research, Byassee assumed that it probably wasn't all that important to growth for a church to be focused on growth as such. "Growth is something you get not by aiming at it," he reasons initially, "but by aiming at something else. Aim at growth and you may get it, you may not, but it's not the goal. The goal is faithfulness to Jesus Christ, a community's life shaped around him, taking part in his redemption of the world. Clear and winsome devotion to that — alignment of a church's budget and hiring and liturgy and attention around Jesus — will fascinate and draw others."

By the end of his research, he decides that while he had been largely right, it also made a real difference to intentionally work to grow. Learning from the researcher David Goodhew, he comes to agree that "churches that intend to grow tend to grow," as Goodhew often notes. Growth is indeed something to aim for, as it focuses efforts on actually reaching out to the surrounding community in imaginative ways, instead of allowing collective energies to be internally-focused and then wondering why new people don't show up. Like a diet, nearly any approach to church growth can work and usually will. The important thing is to try, to learn, and when some initiative inevitably fails, to try again.

Both writers emphasize that no single approach or program is a magic bullet, and that the important thing is to prayerfully seek out what God is calling you to do in your community with your church's particular set of gifts. There is no one size fits all program to follow, except to be truly focused on Christ's saving work, to pray as if you expect that God will show up, and to listen and obey the Spirit's lead.

That said, there are a number of initiatives that God has used to renew congregations time and time again. First and foremost is the Alpha Course, which 24 million people have taken since it started in 1993 at Holy Trinity Brompton. Its creators point out that they never intended it to be an evangelism course, but that's what it became: it was more of a discovery, they like to say, of what God was up to than any forethought on their part. In essence, Alpha walks through the basics of the faith in an 11-week series, with recorded talks over dinner followed by open-ended conversations. Hosts are there to be hospitable, but not to answer anyone's questions: that's left up to the Holy Spirit. Church members are asked to commit to prayer for those taking the course, especially during the Holy Spirit weekend, where inquirers are invited to pray for the Spirit to come into their lives. Many testify that these weekends are where they were met and transformed by Christ.

Messy Church is another C of E initiative that's met wide acclaim, with some 500,000 attending Messy Church services each month in over twenty countries. Unlike Sunday School, which is designed for parents to drop off their kids and go, Messy Church is designed for parents and children to do together: skits, games, snacks, coloring, a kid-friendly lesson, and so on. Several clergy Byassee spoke with said that Messy Church is their best-attended church service of any kind, including their regular Sunday morning worship! Fout relates a statistic told him by Bishop Nic Thorpe, that 40 percent of church growth in England is owed to Messy Church.

Messy Church is only one example of how growing churches in England have gotten creative about building bridges to their communities, serving felt needs, getting out and about instead of simply focusing on building a better Sunday morning experience. Fout and Byassee both describe a number of outward-focused ministries that seek to lower the threshold for getting involved in church, ways of opening the church up to the neighborhood and sending the church out into the neighborhood. Holy Trinity Brompton offers practically-oriented courses on managing finances, marriage, and parenting. "Fresh Expressions" have popped up in thousands of places, praying and worshipping small communities that meet in coffee shops, pubs, homes, and more. Sam Wells, noticing the stream of people who attend St. Martin-in-the-Fields for noon weekday concerts, began offering theological meditations each Thursday on some piece of great sacred music performed by St. Martin's musicians. Now, instead of a poorly attended Thursday Eucharist, he has 250 people attending each week to encounter Christ both in word and the beauty of music.

What makes a church grow? There is much that can be said about this program or that initiative, much of it worthwhile. Finally, what makes a church grow is not any particular program, but the holy fire and passionate love that is behind all of the programs, initiatives, handshakes, and hand-written notes that God is using to renew his Church. If there is a great, all-consuming conviction that the gospel of Jesus Christ is the pearl of great price, worth selling all that we have; if there is a great passion for introducing people to Jesus and a great love that sends us out into the mission fields to see lives transformed, then God's Church will grow. If we have lost our first love, and if our hearts have gone complacent and lukewarm, then the Lord will spew us out of his mouth (Rev. 2:4; 3:16).

But the living God is alive and well in England, filling up old churches that fifty or thirty years ago had dwindled to almost nothing with new life and the fire of the Spirit. God's Spirit can breathe new life into our dry bones, too.

The Rev. Dr. Jordan Hylden is associate rector at the Episcopal Church of the Ascension, Lafayette, Louisiana, where he also serves as a chaplain at Ascension Episcopal School.

TWO

Prayer Drives Congregational Growth

John Deepak Sundara

Kevin Martin's recent article "Who Are We Missing?"[1] highlights a valid sociological and theological commonality among some of the largest congregations in the Episcopal Church: they are theologically and liturgically conservative. This has been documented in various sociology papers: there is a strong connection between membership and Sunday attendance, and historically orthodox theology and traditional liturgy, across mainline traditions, ours included.

By traditional liturgy, I mean a liturgy that is intentionally out

---

1   http://kevinoncong.blogspot.com/2023/01/who-are-we-missing.html

of step with current cultural norms. Indeed, anyone familiar with the three parishes Martin mentions knows that, liturgically, they are all quite different from each other. Although All Souls, Oklahoma City, Church of the Incarnation, Dallas, and St. Martin's, Houston are Rite I parishes, one uses the forms of the 1928 BCP, one is a parish that would have made E.B. Pusey proud, and the other is deeply influenced by the venerable Church of England low-church evangelical, John R.W. Stott.

That being said, it is worth mentioning that, apart from their theological commitments, the rectors of each parish share a particular charism of spiritual leadership, namely a personal discipline of prayer, that lends itself to their congregation's growth and vibrancy, making them outliers in the Episcopal Church. From personal experience, I want to discuss Church of the Incarnation, where I served under the former rector, the Rt. Rev. Anthony Burton, for five and a half years, and St. Martin's, where I now serve under the Rev. Dr. Russell J. Levenson Jr.

First, Bp. Burton. When I served at Church of the Incarnation, the daily rhythm was a morning Mass and Evening Prayer. On the mornings when I made it on time, Bp. Burton was invariably beginning his workday kneeling in prayer. While all of us leafed through the service leaflet, sometimes clumsily, Bp. Burton knew and said it all by heart. It is hard to not remember him kneeling in that chapel. Likewise, when Bp. Burton prayed or celebrated the Mass, every word uttered was simultaneously both his and the prayer book's. Nothing felt rote. The prayers felt true and sincere. He believed every word he prayed.

During the early and painful months of COVID, our parish organized a Zoom Bible study. In the first session, Bp. Burton closed our evening with Compline. I cannot explain how it was possible for one man, praying through his computer, to draw a hundred or so parishioners, also watching and praying through their screens, into a deep moment of faith, peace, and comfort, especially when he prayed these words: "Tend the sick, Lord Christ; give rest to the weary, bless the dying, soothe the suffering, pity the afflicted, shield the joyous; and all for your love's sake." There was something about how he prayed those words, and how they landed on us sitting miles away from him, that I knew this prayer was coming from a priest and bishop whose soul had been deeply shaped, for many decades, by Christ in the school of prayer.

Across the highway from Incarnation is a neighborhood with a community housing project. Over the years, Incarnation has sought to partner with existing ministries and churches in the area, many of which are historical African American congregations and outreach ministries from a variety of traditions. One tragic evening, a drive-by shooting claimed the lives of many innocents, including a child. Residents rallied to support each other through prayer and worship. Their pastors invited Bp. Burton to participate and pray. In a space full of non-white Christians, one would have imagined that Bp. Burton stood out like a sore thumb — a tall, slim, Anglo-Catholic bishop and rector of a predominantly well-to-do, white church. But the pastors invited him for a reason. And Bp. Burton's prayers and words, steeped by decades of prayer book spirituality and piety, were met with resounding amens over and over and over again. There was something about his spiritual leadership that was deeply influenced by his spiritual discipline of daily prayer.

But this trait isn't only evident in Bp. Burton. In one of my first interviews with Russ, I met him at his home, early in the morning. At one of his side tables in his living room was his cup of coffee, his well-worn Bible, and his prayer book. He told me about the gems he had mined in his time with the Lord that morning. During his morning quiet times, he would also sense the Lord prodding him in certain directions about decisions for the life of the parish. Later, I discovered that Russ designates certain topics for each day of the week. For example, on Mondays he prays for all 200 employees of St. Martin's by name.

Russ has a reputation for compelling preaching. I believe this is the secret: while the hymn before the Gospel is still being sung, and before Russ climbs the stairs to the pulpit, he kneels in prayer at his preacher's seat. It feels a tad bit out of step with everything else going around liturgically. And then, after he's done preaching, while we're all reciting the Nicene Creed, Russ is again kneeling in prayer, at his seat. Or sometimes he's off to the vesting room. The lay servers sometimes ask, "Where's Russ off to?" To pray! It should be utterly unsurprising — but it still surprises me — that people give their life to Christ after he has preached.

Of course, God is going to honor the prayers of a priest who hopes his words bear gospel fruit for the sake of Christ's kingdom through the power of the Holy Spirit. This is why people love Russ's preaching. Not least because he is a compelling preacher; but rather that he prays the Holy Spirit compels them — and he does!

Not too long ago, St. Martin's beloved choir conductor died quite suddenly. More than being a conductor, he was a chaplain and pastor to dozens of choir members. The church was mired in a sense of shock and grief. One evening, when all the choir had gathered to mourn, Russ pulled out the prayer book and prayed for us and with us. Once again, every word uttered was simultaneously both his and the prayer book's. Nothing felt rote. The prayers felt true and sincere. He believed every word he prayed. And then we sang a hymn. I hope you see a picture.

The prayer lives and personal disciplines of Bp. Burton and Russ look quite different. Yet, both have deep lives of prayer shaped by the prayer book. And I can't help but conclude that their disciplines, habits, and lives of prayer have much to do with the growth and vibrancy of their congregations.

The Rev. John D. Sundara is the Vicar for Worship and Evangelism at St. Martin's Episcopal Church, Houston, TX.

THREE

Alternative Facts on Church Growth

Benjamin M. Guyer

On November 30, House of Deputies theologian Scott MacDougall published "The Church Is Not Dying, It Is Changing: A Message from the House of Deputies Theologian."[1] MacDougall believes that the decline of the Episcopal Church is overexaggerated and he wants to give Episcopal parishes hope in the Advent season. He opens his short essay by writing, "As leaders in the Episcopal Church, you have all heard a good deal about the *so-called* 'decline of the church'" (emphasis mine). He notes that both membership and financial contributions have been "decreasing for decades," but he fears that "paying too much attention to this narrative of decline may, in fact, be contributing to that decline itself." It's an interesting point, and one worthy of further analysis, but even if true, MacDougall's essay, at best, risks

---

1   https://houseofdeputies.org/2021/11/30/the-church-is-not-dying-it-is-changing-a-message-from-the-house-of-deputies-theologian/

encouraging Episcopalians to ignore the facts of our current state.

ALTERNATIVE FACTS

MacDougall makes two questionable claims. He first argues that "Individual congregations and even some dioceses *are* growing." Second, he writes, "Why are the congregations that are growing growing? Because they realize the church is not *dying*, it is *changing*." No evidence is offered for either assertion, so I will address them in turn.

First, there is no clear evidence that any diocese in the Episcopal Church is growing. Consider the Episcopal Church's information on Average Sunday Attendance by Province and Diocese 2011-2020[2]. Every single diocese saw declines in average Sunday attendance (ASA) during this decade. In the Episcopal Church as a whole, ASA declined by a stunning 30.8 percent. (If you want to see a visual presentation of the data, the Episcopal Church has a fantastic dashboard on point. And, if you are interested in how COVID has affected both attendance and data on point, see Kirk Peterson's helpful article.[3]) Ergo, even if individual congregations are growing, it isn't enough to offset diocesan decline.

If you don't want to use ASA as a metric for growth (or, rather, decline), you could look instead at the Episcopal Church's data on baptized members[4]. Of the church's 111 dioceses, baptized membership declined in 106 dioceses during the same decade. The five exceptions are the dioceses of Haiti (increased by 12.6 percent), Pittsburgh (in-

---

2   https://extranet.generalconvention.org/staff/files/download/30690

3   https://livingchurch.org/commentary/pandemic-skews-parochial-report-data/

4   https://extranet.generalconvention.org/staff/files/download/30689

creased by 1.6 percent), Tennessee (increased by 1.5 percent), the Navajo Missions (increased by 9.9 percent), and Taiwan (increased by 2.9 percent). Yet, even with an increase in baptized members, Sunday attendance in these same five dioceses still decreased. What is more, despite these comparatively small success stories, between 2011 and 2020 overall baptized membership declined by 17.2 percent in the wider Episcopal Church. The claim that some dioceses are growing is correct only as a technicality that privileges baptized members (in only five dioceses!) over and above those who actually attend church.

MacDougall's second claim is that growth happens where people "realize the church is not dying, it is changing." But he offers no evidence that Haiti, Pittsburgh, Tennessee, Navajo Missions, and Taiwan agree with this claim. Nor does he offer any sort of discussion of how "change" (a regrettably vague term) is being used to facilitate growth, whether in these five dioceses or elsewhere. Assuming the best (do you see, dear reader, how charitable I can be?), appealing to "change" is well-intentioned. But we need an analytic deep dive into the precise content of change before we hold it up as a matter for parochial and denominational assurance. (And it may be ethnographers and statisticians, rather than theologians, who are best positioned for this sort of analysis.)

BUT WAIT — LOOK OVER THERE! AND OVER THERE! AND ELSEWHERE, TOO!

Another problem with MacDougall's essay is that its comparative framework is misleading. Referencing PEW Research, he writes, "no denomination — no, not even the evangelical ones — is experiencing explosive growth." This may be true (although some recent evidence suggests that evangelicalism is growing, at the very least as a share of American Christianity), but noting evangelicals' lack of growth explains nothing about the current state of the Episcopal Church. So, let's use PEW's research to unpack larger questions of growth and decline in the United States more broadly, and then use this to see where the Episcopal Church stands.

In 2019, PEW reported that between 2007 and 2019, the number of self-identified Catholics had declined by 4 percent, self-identified Protestants had declined by 8 percent, and, regular Sunday attendance had dropped by 9 percent. By way of comparison, between 2007 and 2019, baptized membership in the Episcopal Church decreased by 21.3 percent, and ASA decreased by 28.8 percent. (Data on the Episcopal Church's ASA between 2007 and 2017[5], as well as baptized members during these years[6], are available online.) I suspect that our decline is, in fact, far bigger than indicated by our waning number of baptized members; religious self-identification, which PEW uses, is a better metric than baptized membership because the latter only matters if you identify with it. As David Goodhew has observed, if current trends continue, the Episcopal Church will have effectively disappeared by 2050.[7]

Pointing to smaller declines among other religious groups does not explain why the Episcopal Church is declining so much more rapidly. Our denomination has chosen to defer much of its intellectual work to a professional class called "theologians." And while it is im-

---

5   https://extranet.generalconvention.org/staff/files/download/26493

6   https://extranet.generalconvention.org/staff/files/download/26497

7   https://livingchurch.org/covenant/the-episcopal-church-in-2050/

portant to set these developments within a theological context, this theological context must also be informed by responsible use of the data.

SO... WHAT?

Before offering a recommendation, allow me to sound three notes of caution. First, there is a popular claim among conservatives which asserts that more traditional forms of belief cause churches to grow. I am skeptical of this view for two reasons. First, I have seen no data which offer anything other than correlations between theology and growth in select instances (e.g., the growth of Orthodox churches in the English-speaking world). Second, even if traditional forms of orthodoxy sometimes correlate with growth, at the macro level, even conservative churches are declining — although they are not declining anywhere near as quickly as, e.g., the Episcopal Church. Finally, neither of the first two points here should be used to deny the fact that significant hemorrhages in membership have occurred due to the Episcopal Church's adoption of "progressive" positions at variance with a wider, more "conservative," Christian consensus.

So, I'm going to suggest that, from here on out, it should be every diocese for itself. Let alliances be made and self-selected forms of cooperation ensue, and do not interfere with those who choose a way more "conservative" or more "progressive" than your own. General Convention should be delayed for a decade. General Convention is part of the bene esse (wellbeing), rather than part of the esse (essence), of the Episcopal Church. It is massively expensive, hugely time consuming (and thus quite exclusionary of many, if not most, laity), and there is little reason to have big, expensive meetings with attendance nearing free fall. A period of ecclesial disorganization is not desirable, but it is far preferable to permanent dissolution. We must now live an ecclesiology of emergency.

CONCLUSION

No institution deserves to survive. Christians are so very foolish in believing that, if they do the right thing, God will take their side and make up the difference. But let us open our eyes. Even if Word and Sacrament remain means of grace, the deity is otherwise silent. The theatre of history is, at present, a testament only to our own choices. The fundamental task of ecclesiastical historians today has become that of preparing to write epitaphs — and that will involve far more truth telling than is currently on offer.

Dr. Benjamin Guyer is a lecturer in the department of history and philosophy at the University of Tennessee at Martin. His monograph How the English Reformation was Named: The Politics of History, 1400-1700 *is forthcoming from Oxford University Press. He is the co-editor with Paul Avis of* The Lambeth Conference: Theology, History, Polity and Purpose *(Bloomsbury, 2017).*

FOUR

A Theology for Anglican Church Growth

David Goodhew

"It's just an unspiritual bigging yourself up." This was the acerbic verdict of one Durham ordinand on the subject of church growth. His hostility to talking of growing churches is widely shared, at least in the Global North. When two or three clerics are gathered together and the subject of church growth comes up, a multitude of theological objections rapidly appear: It's the kingdom that matters, not numerical growth; It's an ungodly sidelining of the need to love one's neighbor; Isn't church growth just something those uncouth schismatics obsess about?

These are serious objections, but beyond them, there is often a lurking sense of other fears. For many parish priests in North America, Britain, and much of the West there is a troubling worry that looking for numerical church growth is not only theologically dodgy but also practically futile. In the Western world, nearly every media and academic outlet trumpets the decline of Christianity. When many parishes and even whole dioceses are being spliced together because of their decline, looking to expand congregations can seem like wishful thinking.

There is some value in wariness of church growth. It *can* be an unspiritual bigging yourself up. But the reverse is also true. When Anglicans in the United States and Britain disdain "mere" numerical growth, as attendance in many dioceses drops, there is a certain convenience in the assumption that decline is inevitable. Anglican disdain for church growth is ecclesiological palliative care.

I want to sketch the outline of a possible theology for Anglican church growth. It is not original, being drawn largely on the work of others. A nuanced theology of church growth is possible but also necessary. The growth that churches in the Global North so urgently need cannot come unless there is a robust theology beneath it.

CHURCH GROWTH IS BIBLICAL

If, just for a moment, we move the Gospel of Luke after the Gospel of John, we see immediately the nature of Luke's two-part work. At its heart is the resurrection of Jesus: the end point of Luke's Gospel and the starting point of Acts. The first part of Luke's work is suffused with talk of the kingdom; yet in the book of Acts, kingdom is mentioned relatively rarely. This does not mean that the theme is eclipsed, but the primary way in which the kingdom is expressed in the world after the Ascension of Jesus is by the formation of local churches.

More than a few theologians downplay the local church as something second-rate compared to the kingdom. The New Testament knows nothing of this. Indeed, the Book of Acts is punctuated by a series of summaries by Luke that note the numerical growth of the Church (6:7; 9:31; 12:24; 16:5; 19:20). Most moving of all are those points when the apostles arrive at places like Tyre and Puteoli and find a community of believers *already* there. The obvious inference is that unnamed Christians carried the gospel there. These unnamed Christians were quite possibly not apostles, but they were acting apostolically. They challenge us to go and do likewise.

CHURCH GROWTH IS DOCTRINALLY NECESSARY

A theological basis for seeking numerical church growth is readily to hand in Scripture. But it is not quite so obvious when we turn to doctrine. Here the work of writers such as professors Alister McGrath and Ivor Davidson and of Bishop Graham Tomlin is immensely helpful.[1] They point us to how the fundamental doctrines of Incarnation, Atonement, and Trinity call us to an extrovert faith, which seeks the growth and proliferation of communities that incarnate the gospel in every community.

Graham Tomlin argues that when we look at the Spirit, we see a

---

1   These writers, alongside other key scholars, discuss what constitutes a nuanced theology of church growth in David Goodhew (ed.), *Towards a Theology of Church Growth*, (Routledge 2015).

God whose essence is sending:

> Theologically speaking, mission and the consequent
> growth of the church begin with the begetting of
> the Son and the procession of the Spirit from the
> Father. It starts with the Trinitarian life of God be-
> fore it ever involves the creation, let alone the hu-
> man part of that creation.[2]

In saying this, Tomlin commends the importance of a full-blood-ed pneumatology. But he is also alert to the way we can sometimes fall into an idolatrous assumption that the Spirit can be controlled by humans. Tomlin sees the tension in seeing the Holy Spirit as free from human control yet given freely by God as akin to the tension between seeing church growth as in the hands of God yet requiring committed human effort if it is to come to pass. For Tomlin, the practice of in-voking the Holy Spirit is the way of managing this tension. By asking continually for the Holy Spirit we have access to him, but our need to ask means we cannot ever control him.

Tomlin also stresses that suffering is intrinsic to such a ministry. Any pneumatology has to be a *pneumatologia crucis*. This is the cru-cial underpinning for growing churches. This is cross-shaped minis-try, *rooted in suffering, not in neo-liberal paradigms of what constitutes success. Growing churches means taking up the cross.* Emphasis on the Holy Spirit requires that emphasis on numerical growth be balanced by desire to grow in personal holiness and in service to society. The Holy Spirit grows congregations, *but also* grows people by maturing

---

2   Graham Tomlin, 'The Prodigal Spirit and Church Growth', Ibid., p. 136.

them and by healing them.

That is why church growth matters. Healthy well-functioning churches are places where people can be restored and become agents of change and renewal within the world beyond the church. The reason we need churches to grow is not to pay the bills, or to feel good about ourselves. It is to enable humanity, in tune with the Spirit of God, to fulfil its divine calling to care for and nurture the world which God has created.[3]

And to say this is to challenge Anglicans on whether our tendency to shrink may be linked to our failure to invoke the Holy Spirit and our general tendency, like many Western Christians, to downplay the third person of the Trinity.[4]

CHURCH GROWTH IS CENTRAL TO FIDELITY TO TRADITION

In 1800 the population of London was around 1 million. By 1900 it was around 6 million. During the 19th century, huge numbers of Anglican churches were planted by Anglo-Catholics and evangelicals alike. Anglicans have often stood by as modern cities in the United States and Britain rapidly expanded in recent decades, in ways as dramatic as anything the Victorians saw, and failed to emulate our forebears by founding new churches. In our inaction, we are being unfaithful to tradition. Indeed, we engage in a decidedly postmodern worship of the individual, which sees sharing faith as arrogant (although pro-

---

3   Ibid., p. 141.

4   Anglicanism in recent decades has sought a greater emphasis on the Holy Spirit, but it may be questioned whether modern Anglicanism in the Global North has yet arrived at a truly robust pneumatology.

mulgating individualism, for some reason, is never arrogant).

As we look more widely across the Christian tradition, we discover that enthusiasm for church growth was evidenced by some surprising figures. Living in the northeast of England, I rejoice in ancient saints like the seventh-century St. Cuthbert. He is usually depicted as a man of prayer who had a deep communion with nature. This is true, but not the whole truth. Bede tells us how Cuthbert "often did the rounds of the villages, sometimes on horseback, more often on foot, preaching the way of truth to those who had gone astray."[5] Cuthbert sought to grow the Church.

Likewise, St. Francis is portrayed as a man who profoundly loved the poor and God's creation. And he did, but he also loved to share the gospel and build up the Church. The aphorism attributed to St. Francis that one should always preach the gospel but only use words "if necessary" — with its implication that the verbal proclamation of faith is secondary — has become an ecclesial cliché. But the *practice* of St. Francis points in the opposite direction. He and the friars were at the center of intentional Church growth in the Middle Ages.

It is well known that St Francis invented the concept of the Christmas crib: but it is less frequently appreciated that he did so precisely because there was a pressing need for new ways to teach the story of Jesus' nativity to an ill-educated population that knew nothing of the Christian story. The work of evangelism was foundational to the friars. Chapter 12 of St Francis 1223 Rule was devoted to 'regulating and promoting missionary activity'.[6]

---

5   Bede, Life of Cuthbert, chapter 9.

6   Miranda Threlfall-Holmes, "Growing the Mediaeval Church," in Goodhew (ed.), *Towards a Theology of Church Growth*, pp. 188-89.

Thomas Cranmer was deeply concerned that the local church connect with its locality. This was expressed by his passion for liturgy in the language of the people and pastoral use of Scripture to draw people closer to God; hence the role of the "comfortable words" in the prayer book's communion. The power of scriptural rumination and cultural contextualization has much to teach Anglicans today.[7]

CHURCH GROWTH IS REQUIRED BY REASON AND EXPERIENCE

Anthropologist Tanya Luhrmann of Stanford University writes:

> What one might call an avalanche of medical data has demonstrated that, for reasons still poorly understood, those who attend church and believe in God are healthier and happier and live longer that those who do not.[8]

A recent research report details the full extent of this avalanche.[9] It is academically proven that joining a congregation is connected to marked improvement in physical, mental, and relational well-being. In an age when attending church can be seen as a quasi-pathological disorder or optional lifestyle choice, this needs saying.

---

7   See Ashley Null, "Divine Allurement: Thomas Cranmer and Tudor Church Growth," Ibid.

8   Tanya Luhrmann, *When God Talks Back: Understanding the American Evangelical Relationship with God* (Vintage Books, 2012), p. 331.

9   Nick Spencer et al., *Religion and Well Being* (Theos, 2016).

In an age when people love their phones and computers but forget that their phones and computers never love them back[10], Christian congregations are deeply good news, so their growth and proliferation is deeply good news too.

Church growth is not peripheral and it is not optional. When we look outside the Western world, it becomes clear that such growth is also eminently possible. This raises the crucial and disturbing question of whether the decline of many Western churches, not least Anglicanism in the United States and Britain, has some theological roots. When we understand Scripture, doctrine, and tradition as if growing local churches were a side issue, or even something to disdained in favor of supposedly higher kingdom goals, we are not only distorting Scripture, reason, and tradition. We are, arguably, buying into the secular mindset that is the air we breathe.

More and more, I find myself turning to Charles Taylor's bracing diagnosis of our condition. Taylor sees us as living in a secular age. Part of living in a secular age is to assume growing churches is unnecessary or impossible or both. It will take deliberate act, a kind of exodus, to let go of such decline theology. Much of Anglicanism in the Global North suffers from this decline theology, in which the growth of congregations is sidelined or even looked down upon. My friends from the Global South find this a bizarre way in which to understand the world. I think they are right.

A range of research shows that churches that intend to grow tend to grow. And intentionality only comes through theology. Having a nuanced theology of church growth will assist churches in growing

---

10   I take this phrase from Kallistos Ware's *Orthodox Theology in the Twenty-First Century* (Geneva, 2012), p. 26.

numerically, but doing so in a godly way. Such a theology will also inoculate us from the hopeless horizon of secularity that assumes this world is all there is. A theology of Anglican church growth, rooted in the hope of the resurrection, shows us what treasure we have to offer a world of aching loneliness: a community of thoroughly fallible people made strong by the hope of the risen Jesus.

The Rev. Dr. David Goodhew is vicar of St Barnabas Church, Middlesbrough, England and visiting fellow of St John's College, Durham University.

FIVE

Shooting the Messengers?

'Conservative' Theology and Church Growth

Jason Postma

Ideas have legs. Or, if you will, you reap what you sow. The truth of these sayings is nearly universally accepted; their wisdom is incontrovertible — unless you are reacting to a sociological study analyzing the cause of growth and decline in mainline congregations. After a five-year study of 22 congregations, and interviews with over 2,220 congregants and the clergy who serve them, David Haskell, Kevin Flatt, and Stephanie Burgoyne concluded that ideas have legs. More specifically, their study, "Theology Matters,"[1] concluded that congregations that espouse "liberal" theology are declining and congregations that espouse "conservative" theology are growing.

---

1   https://link.springer.com/article/10.1007/s13644-016-0255-4

One would assume that this relatively straightforward conclusion, backed by strong statistical evidence, would be cause for prayerful reflection by congregations of all theological stripes and sizes. A particularly pertinent question for reflection is: How are we, as God's people in this community, being faithful or unfaithful to the traditions we have received? (cf. 2. Thess. 2:15). Like all traditions, Christian tradition is living and breathing and therefore requires careful stewardship and contemplation in every age and culture. Faithfulness matters.

However, once the results of the study were publicized in major publications, responses were often less careful and more visceral. Perhaps unsurprisingly, more reactive responses came from those implicated in ecclesial decline and ranged from outright rejection of the conclusions to suggestive claims about the hidden agendas of the authors, to more relevant questions about the adequacy of sample size and definitions, to attempts to refocus the question away from theology to demographics, to smug chiding of apparently simple-minded conservatives, to outright apathy. After all, *who cares*?

In many ways, these reactions strangely echo that of the tenants in Jesus' parable in Luke 20:9-18; the servants sent by the vineyard owner are beaten and sent away empty-handed. Haskell, Flatt, and Burgoyne could be just those servants. Sometimes it seems as though those laboring in liberal fields are content to continue sowing seed that does not produce a good yield as a matter of principle, regardless of the desires of the vineyard owner. Are liberals, in defiance of their own theology, hoping for a miracle of an abundant yield? Or is a stubborn refusal to repent part of the problem? After all, is "nice people doing nice things" a perfectly acceptable ecclesial *raison d'être* in this day and age?

AND WHAT WILL HAPPEN WHEN THE SON OF THE VINEYARD OR THE VINEYARD OWNER APPEARS?

Liberal churches ought to reflect seriously on this question, as it is posed by the results of the Haskell study. Indeed, liberal reactions of protesting and questioning the conclusions of the study could be counted as evidence that the conclusions are indeed accurate, indicative of a failure to reflect prayerfully upon a potential word from the Lord. Nevertheless, the Word of God comes to us both as judgment and, therefore, mercy.

Conservative churches, on the other hand, cannot simply respond to the study's results with a smug sense of superiority.[2] It doesn't tell the whole story. There remain theologically orthodox congregations that are not experiencing numerical growth, despite having sound preaching, top-notch music, and excellent discipleship programs.[3] Moreover, conservative congregations that *are* growing should reflect on the sources of their growth: Is it from robust and winsome evangelism? Or do marketing gimmicks explain their success? Or are they merely the benefactors of ecclesial attrition? The latter two situations are hardly causes for celebration; they are causes for repentance.

---

2   Nor should they simply accept the entire study at face value. For example, the authors' definition of the "factual" understanding of Scripture is theologically problematic, as are their definitions of "liberal" and "conservative."

3   Moreover, there are also liberal congregations that are growing numerically. However, at this point it is important to remind ourselves that anecdotal evidence cannot override statistical evidence, our desires to the contrary notwithstanding.

AND WHAT WILL HAPPEN WHEN THE SON OF THE VINEYARD OR THE VINEYARD OWNER APPEARS?

Conservative churches cannot be lulled into complacency but must seriously reflect on this question as it is posed by the results of the Haskell study. The refusal to do so will ensure that this word will fall on deaf ears and conservative churches will find themselves in exile alongside their liberal sisters and brothers. The Word of God comes to us as judgment, and, therefore, mercy.

Mainline churches in North America, liberal and conservative alike, are slowly awakening to the realization that the days of cultural Christendom are over. For some, this is a cause for anxiety; the result is a desperate attempt to stay in sync with culture, even if it means jettisoning core elements of the Church's traditions and teachings.[4] For others, post-Christendom is a cause for celebration, as though we can *finally* get on with the work of the Church without the hindrance of excess cultural baggage.[5]

The post-Christendom situation of the Church need not be complex. If it is true that theology matters, that ideas have legs, that we reap what we sow, then the focus of the church moving into the future is as simple as keeping and sharing the faith as we've received it without cultural accommodation or rejection. Of course, this is easier said than done, but I find great encouragement in knowing that it can be

---

4   For some others, the rise of secularization in post-Christendom is a cause for celebration because it means liberation from outdated and irrelevant traditions. Cf. for example, the work of John Shelby Spong.

5   For others, post-Christendom means that the church has to reclaim the culture in order to restore it to proper godly order.

done. The conclusions of "Theology Matters" indicate as much.

Those who have ears to hear, let them hear.

The Rev. Jason Postma is assistant curate to the rector in the Regional Ministry of Saugeen Shores, Tara, and Chatsworth.

SIX

The Episcopal Church Must be Made Stronger in the Hinterland

Chip Prehn

"Many hands make light work." I reflected on this maxim last weekend when I discovered fire-ant mounds all over my yard. This time of year, when it has rained in the semi-arid Southwest, fire ants of a sudden build these veritable castles. Hundreds, probably thousands, of them carefully assemble the edifices from various kinds of soil they manipulate and process. Tiny pieces of rock are also used here and there, I think to give weight to the vaulted ceilings against the elements. They build palaces one piece at a time, each ant doing his or her part. Some of the ant castles are colossal.

Since I do not want the mounds scattered on my lawn, I stir through them with a stick, or spray them away with a garden hose, or I impose birth control by way of a mix that stops the growth of the empire by killing the queens. When the queen is gone, the rest of the realm loses its purpose. Only when I am forced to destroy a mound can I see the intricate interior architecture of the finely engineered buildings. Look what these creatures can do when they work together! I thought of the old cartoon where ants invade a happy picnic and, combining forces, take up a large roasted turkey and transport it homeward.

The ants prove that there is strength in numbers. This prompted me to remember the spectacle of Dunkirk in 1940, when several hundred little boats crossed the English Channel to save the British army backed onto the beach by the Germans. The rescue of thousands of troops was made possible by many individuals — fishermen, small-contract shippers, leisure-boat skippers — working together toward that single goal. This event leading up to the Battle of Britain is often called a miracle. There are other examples of such strength-in-numbers miracles, such as the way hundreds of people passing sandbags can prevent high water from destroying homes, or recall the once common bucket brigade: many people passing buckets of water to put out a big fire. "Many hands make light work."

Like most churches, the Episcopal Church likes the strength of numbers. Good numbers in a particular church — communicant count and good annual giving — are surely signs of life, health, and strength. The *obvious* number strength is what the Dunkirk deliverers and the ants have. My home parish in a large healthy city is moving toward 10,000 souls. What an Episcopal church of this size can do is amazing. What I'm calling obvious number strength is strength indeed! (I would also note that the 20-year rector who built up that formerly C of E parish — may God rest his soul in peace — was adamant that *quality* and not quantity must be the goal.)

But the Church ought to be cautious of using numbers such as these to measure the quality of our work. We can decide to assess our progress by reckoning upon a different number. There is an *unobvious* number strength that measures success, not by ASA or the size of a budget, but by counting the *total churches* in a statistical or demographic sample.

If we count up the hundreds of Episcopal churches in small towns and rural areas from Maine to Alaska, from North Dakota to Key West, the number is surprising and impressive. These often tiny churches lack the obvious number strength of many big-city and suburban churches, but together — as a group — they make an extremely important witness in the hinterland. Reckoning by way of the number of parishes and missions — small as they usually are — instead of "communicant strength" allows us to discover to our surprise an Episcopal Church stronger than we supposed. As with green bell peppers in a garden, it is quite easy to miss the strong presence of little churches in the hinterland, but they are there.

I have been something of a country vicar for the last three years. In addition to my professional work as an educational consultant, I do Sunday supply. I am half the year in the Texas Hill Country and half in the Shenandoah Valley of Virginia. In the Old Dominion, I am a circuit rider serving small congregations all over the place. In Texas, I am vicar of one community called St. Mark's Church, Coleman. Serving churches in small-town America has opened a whole new world for me. Growing up in large parishes in two big cities, and being overly proud of what I possessed, I was mostly ignorant of what goes on in small-town and rural parishes. I had no idea what these churches must deal with year in and year out — and yet they have been delivering Anglican faith and practice for three and sometimes four centuries.

At Coleman, we have gained two persons in two years to improve our ASA to 22. A young couple with five children is coming in July. Our ASA will thus rise again! We broke records on Christmas Eve and Easter Day this year: 63 and 84, respectively. The beautiful little brick church, entirely carpenter gothic on the inside, is especially pretty when it is full of people. The building is as neat as a pin. The memorial garden is peaceful and pretty. The lawn is always mown, we have a new outdoor pavilion and sidewalk. One could eat off the floor of the parish hall. St. Mark's people love the Lord, love their church, take good care of the place, and look after one another in and out of season. They are also proud Episcopalians and utterly determined to keep their Christian community up and running. There is no debt.

Most St. Mark's people are ranchers or have jobs related in some manner to ranching or farming. Even the enterprising lady who runs a splendid gift shop sells as much to locals as to tourists. Several of our parishioners come to church redolent of the cattle business. They have been up feeding since before dawn. But their stories transcend pinkeye, escaped calves, broken fences, and lack of grass. They also tell stories of reading the prayer book to a sick friend, of working at the homeless shelter in town, of preparing meals for the street people (O yes! even in Coleman), or preparing for and leading Morning Prayer services between the eucharistic Sundays.

Our little church has an "organist" every Sunday of the year. We use an MP3 device that gives us a pipe organ (more or less). All of us would prefer a live musician, but that's not worked out. Whoever did the digital recordings must be a Methodist, since a *Hymnal 1982* selection will suddenly stop after just three verses. But we do fine.

The churches I serve in Virginia are small but very busy and happy places. Again, they are neat, clean, and debt-free. The people are eager to practice their faith. One congregation has been waiting for its new rector for two years because he is English and a federal government that will allow millions of foreigners to cross the border without credentials of any sort has made this British cleric sweat it out like a suspected terrorist.

I serve another country church that can afford a supply priest only once a month. It does a first-class Morning Prayer service the rest of the time. The usual lectors have a great reverence for the Scriptures and respect for the English language. A little church not far from our farm is one of the most beautiful stone churches I have ever seen. When you go inside, you are instantly in a world of jewel-like colors that invite you into the realm of the beautiful God. A spotless carpet takes you forward to the chancel area, replete with polished silver and brass. Everything is in its place. The perennial warden of this church is the organist. He is really good on the bench, picks hymns he knows the choir — that is, the whole congregation — can sing, and has the pastoral touch. In truth, he is the pastor of the church. The ASA at this stone church is probably 17. The annual budget is not above $35,000. Yet parishioners give till it hurts to various charitable causes in the area. They are staunch Episcopalians of the more traditional sort and are thus suspicious of innovations in religion if they are rooted in ideology and not theology. Their commitment and their discipline are impressive.

Back out in Coleman, the bishop visited us last December. He was extremely pleased to confirm four young adults. They are the finest young persons I've ever met. (I am a former priest-educator, so I have known a great many teenagers.) I realize that conscientious, hard-working children and youth can gain a great education anywhere in any sort of school if the right ingredients are there. I know that huge, well-fixed schools in the big cities have incredible offerings and boast remarkable data. On the other hand, I believe that if a teenager does not live in a big urban area or is unable to go away to a good church school, the next best thing is to gain one's education in small-town schools. The reason is that the same person is expected to do many things. You've seen the picture of the football player with the homecoming queen on one arm and a trumpet in the other. That boy and that girl are gaining a multitude of experiences in that little high school that will serve them and others for life.

My point here is that the four deeply formed, impressive youth we presented for confirmation at St. Mark's Church last December *are now strong Episcopal laity* who will serve in various ministries and carry on the Anglican tradition in rural and other parts of America. They grew up on ranches. They will likely remain in the area and practice their religion *as Episcopalians*. Quantity does not mean quality. Presiding Bishop John Maury Allin grew up in a small-town parish where he and a girl were the only two children in the Sunday school for years. She went on to run an Episcopal religious order.

I must not paint too rosy a picture. Small-town and rural America face a plethora of challenges. Not a few of these challenges have been created by both political parties, which have been rather stupid in terms of agriculture policies, especially as sustainability becomes imperative. In some areas, commitment to monoculture has ruined the soil. Trade policies in Washington have put a lot of ranchers and farmers out of business. There is plenty of poverty in rural areas. Opioid addiction has decimated the Shenandoah Valley and many other parts of small-town and rural America.

I am likewise deeply anxious about how the current political divisions in the United States — is it not in part a city *versus* country dynamic? — may affect TEC's attitude about and support of hinterland parishes and missions. Just when TEC needs this non-urban witness the most, and just when the hinterland churches need the support of TEC the most, the larger, better-off body appears aloof and often indifferent. I wonder if we are facing the same large challenge the Domestic and Foreign Missionary Society of the Protestant Episcopal Church in the USA faced in the early 19th century? Other Christian bodies are *way* ahead of us. Not only the Baptists, Church of Christ, and independent evangelical communities, but the Roman Catholic Church has made a huge commitment to the hinterland. Some of the prettiest RC churches in the world are in the middle of nowhere, which of course is somewhere. The Mormons are committed too, and paganism thrives in the forests, deserts, and one-horse towns. Where is the Episcopal Church?

If we believe the gospel is true; if we believe that Christianity offers the most compelling perspective of the purpose of this life, and the historically best path through mortal existence; and if we believe that Anglican Christianity has an excellence and a beauty worth sharing, then we must get a strategy and derive tactics from it in order to "weigh in" in small towns and rural areas. The Episcopal Church is in fact getting good exposure *outside* the metropolises, but the witness needs more concerted effort and financial support from the larger body. Perhaps Christianity itself will go rural and will thrive in small churches with a few people. This has happened quite often in the last 2,000 years.

As an Episcopalian, I want to have "coverage" across the land and not just in certain parts of the land. If city fellers from other religious backgrounds find Anglicanism a rather compelling phenomenon, then hinterland folk might also find TEC a happy home. We must tell them more about it. There is no Episcopal church in Kaycee, Wyoming, or Crosby, Mississippi, but there could be. I'll wager that God has already given the charism of headship to someone in these and other small communities. We might reach out to these leaders, offer a little theological education (but, please, not too much!), get them some practical training, and get out of their way. These folks belong to us and practice the same Faith via different pieties. Most country people I know admire our presiding bishop and welcome all sorts of strangers. Small towns and rural areas are no less human than metropolitan areas. While many of the people with whom I worship on most Sundays are concerned that TEC has become the Democratic Party at prayer, they are not going anywhere and really are committed to the idea that in Christ Jesus there is a unity of truth.

"Many hands make light work." Small American churches make a contribution to the advance of the gospel that is much "bigger" than the size of a congregation indicates. While it is still true that these small platoons are located in areas losing net population, things may be changing a bit. The Great Panic of 2020 (i.e., COVID) has driven hundreds of thousands of people out of the cities into the country. In any case, there is great potential in rural and small-town America, and we must think again about the opportunity. The part little churches play in the Christian witness in America — unobvious number strength — is way over and above what their ASA and budgets would indicate. Taken as a group, these little churches have a large effect.

I submit that we should make it a priority to help them remain in the saddle against the odds. These people are masters of thrift, creativity, and imagination. Their presence in the villages, small towns, and little cities of our country is often a blessing for the local communities and is a living reminder that Anglican Christianity is not dead, gone, and forgotten. But they could use a little boost. We can give it to them. This would be a way to practice our belief that the gospel of Jesus Christ is true for all, anywhere.

The Rev. Dr. W.L. (Chip) Prehn is president of The Living Church Foundation and is a principal of Dudley & Prehn Educational Consultants. He was a parish priest for 12 years before turning to school administration and consulting. Prehn writes poetry, fiction, nonfiction, and history.

SEVEN

Seen and Unseen:

Unveiling and Addressing A Hidden Obstacle to Church Renewal

Mark Edington

Whatever accounts for our character and institutions will also account for our values, which themselves belong to, and are effective and intelligible at, only their own specific stage in human history.

— Isaiah Berlin, "The Philosophy of Giambattista Vico," in *Three Critics of the Enlightenment*

People of goodwill can (and do) disagree over two basic questions confronting the church today: Why is the church declining in numbers, and what ought to be done about it? Of course, one's answer to the second question typically depends on one's answer to the first. Diagnosis typically determines treatment. And not surprisingly, the interpretive lenses one brings to both questions have an important role in determining what one sees.

It can hardly be surprising that a church centered on a common text called the Book of Common Prayer would look for liturgical answers to sociological questions; neither it is too surprising that we, like most any other gathering of people in our increasingly polarized society, are certain that outcomes must surely follow convictions — or, to say it differently, that orthodoxy (or ortho-advocacy) leads to flourishing, and that (conversely) the absence of flourishing is evidence of that our theology is poorly founded, our positions are questionable, or our advocacy misguided.

But of course, to say that we look to liturgy and proclamation for explanations of our predicament — once we agree, if we even can, on just what our predicament is — may be to begin by privileging our preferences in the first place. Theologians believe the answer to our challenge is more (or more rigorous) theology; liturgists believe it must, of course, be better (and certainly more!) liturgy; activists believe the answer is more activism. Nails abound in the world for those who wield hammers.

In all of this, we are not so much distinguishing ourselves from, but in some basic way only reenacting, the divisions in our broader society. That ought to be the first sign that our efforts to align ourselves more closely with God's ongoing mission in the world are in some way already caught up, and hijacked by, predictable — and predictably misleading — ways of thinking.

Social psychologists teach us that we all have an "appraisal tendency" — a way of seeing the world fundamentally shaped by unique and largely unconscious preferences and emotional predispositions. They teach us that unless we are careful, our appraisal tendencies can limit, in some cases severely, our reality.

It may just be that an organizing principle of a community like the church is that it gathers together people sharing a similar appraisal tendency — because, of course, they see the same reality in largely the same way. And that, in consequence, means that they are limited in the same way as well, sharing in heated agreement an incomplete view of the world.

Christian humility should teach us that not only are we sometimes not quite right in our conclusions but in our thinking; and that should invite us to wonder — what might we be missing, or not seeing, that is actually shaping our circumstances in important ways? What are the unseen things that may be determining our course in significant ways — perhaps even more profoundly than the things that naturally attract our attention and antagonism?

This short note proposes a somewhat different focus for our conversation about the circumstances of our church, one that might disclose different reasons why we seem to struggle with adapting to the future God is calling us into. It is one that will surely not be surprising — but one that, like all polite families of good breeding, we do not discuss because of our respect for the virtue of modesty. But it is exactly this resulting invisibility causing us to miss something that might have even greater significance than the things we prefer to focus on

— witness and worship — in shaping the horizon of our possibilities.

I will here propose a different cause for our observed circumstance of decline, and a different cause for our seeming struggle to respond to difficult challenges as earlier generations of the church did. I'll then offer a way of thinking and speaking about the church we are now called to be, one that consciously articulates a vision centered on the model of the early church that is at odds with the culture around us — and with the institutions that we have inherited in the church we have received.

A DIFFERENT KIND OF CLIMATE CHANGE

Think for a moment about the deepening polarization in our society — something political scientists are now urgently drawing attention to, with warnings about the threats to the very foundations of democracy in the United States. We surely know something in our church about how polarization can fracture institutions, destroy communities, and harm human relationships.

Yet beneath and subtending all this is a deeper change in the United States that may fairly be seen as creating the conditions upon which all this rests. I am speaking of the growing division in economic possibilities and outcomes for both individuals and communities. It is not just that income inequality has increased (it has); it is not just that social mobility, the chance that any of us will have a path toward a better and more economically secure future than the generation before us has decreased (it also has).

It is not just that the aggregate distribution of income in the United States has shifted drastically away from middle-income families to wealthy families in the past fifty years. Beyond this, and perhaps even more important in terms of driving the forces of social estrangement, is the fact that this same pattern of growing inequality — and hence a decline in the sense of common purpose or destiny — has taken place in social institutions as well. And the church has been no less affected.

While the full lessons of the COVID-19 pandemic for the church are yet to be determined, one thing seems a certainty beyond dispute: The pandemic laid bare the inequality that characterizes the life of the church in the early twenty-first century. When even an outlet like *The Economist* observes that "lockdown has turned Christianity into a winner-take-all business," something is happening that perhaps we ought to be paying attention to.

Numbers may not be as compelling to us, given our appraisal tendencies, as prophetic pronouncement or liturgical practice. But the data available to us by means of that humblest of all duties of the annual cycle of the church's life, the Parochial Report, tell a story of how our church is caught up in this wrenching trend of greater inequality — and cast light on the challenges we face in proving to be a church able to respond with grace, joy, and both a common purpose and common prayer in meeting the challenges ahead of us.

The investment figures shown in the Parochial Report come from two sources. The first is the good offices of the Executive Office of the General Convention, and in particular those sainted people who gently remind us every year, sometimes repeatedly, to submit our reports. What this data shows is that the total of all reported endowment funds across all 3,202 reporting parishes of the Episcopal Church was $4,933,691,305 in 2019 — the last full pre-pandemic calendar year — and $5,421,648,478 in 2020, a growth rate of 9.89 percent. (By contrast, the Standard & Poor's 500 index grew by 15 percent in that same period; church endowments are conservatively managed.)

The table shows the top fifty endowments of individual parishes, ranked in descending order, as reported on line 20 of the "Stewardship and Financial Information of the Reporting Congregation" section of the Parochial Report. The data disclose the reality beneath the sense that the pandemic exposed the inequalities among; these fifty churches account for nearly twenty-three percent of all endowed funds held by all 6,376 parishes in the Episcopal Church. Or, to say it in different terms, *one half of one percent of all Episcopal parishes — that is to say, just 32 churches — hold nearly a fifth (18 percent) of all endowed parochial funds in the church.*

Is this the church we are called to be? I suggest that this inequality — or, more accurately, the inability of our governing structures and patterns of work to unlock the potential within it — is more significant in hindering our ability to respond with grace and effective ministry to God's call to us across the future than those things that more naturally capture our attention and passion. But beneath that observation is an unsettling question: Is there something about the structures of the church we have inherited, and the values it enshrines, that have in some ways contributed to this outcome? And if so, how should we think about these things?

One might say, in view of all this — and some have — that the proper response in this moment is to adopt an attitude of "every diocese for itself." Of course, it is a short move from that position to a neoliberal rule of self-help and survival of the fittest — every *church* for itself. But it is hard to see how such a view can possibly be aligned with the scriptural challenge of Acts 4; and if we are to be a church following the pattern of the apostolic church — and that church, let it be said, adapted with profound capacity for innovation to a rapidly changing world, as did the Episcopal Church itself in earlier generations — then we must reject that counsel outright for what it is, a case of irenicism with the dominant culture we are called not to conform to, but convert.

THE CHURCH AS COMMONWEAL

The experience of the Episcopal Church in Europe points toward a different possibility. We are a part of the church that simply could not exist without the support of the wider church. Our sense of dependence on and interdependence with the larger church makes us more alive, as disciples, to the notion — sometimes, let's face it, abstract to Episcopalians — of our dependence on God. As an organic part of the church living under the necessity of invention and adaptation, as a place where experimentation is both our condition and our charism, for us to be "Episcopal" means in a very real way to be in a relationship of commonweal with each other, and with the whole church.

For us, God's call to us in mission across the years ahead — the vision we sense and the voice we follow that leads to vitality in spirit and growth in service — is *the Church as Commonweal*.

There is good news in the story of this data. There is tremendously good work going on, and good being done by some of those parishes blessed to be at the wealthy end of the distribution spectrum. Many of those who have been given talents are about the work of investing them. What is more, they are setting models for how best to effectively and accountably invest those talents for the benefit of communities worldwide.

What is needed is a means by which to engage the one percent of our churches in a virtuous competition — and collaboration — to identify, encourage, and spread practices and initiatives helping the whole church to thrive in a changed world. For while it is true that all faith communities, ours included, have entered a period of numeric decline, it is not true that all our communities are declining. There are green shoots and signs of life, often in the least likely and most overlooked places. We have the capacity to find them, help them flourish, and share their example with others.

Are we really resigned to the values that lead us toward an every-church-for-itself church? Or are we prepared to live into the challenge — perhaps the call — of the Church as Commonweal? Surely there is a sufficient well of imagination and innovation among the One Percent of our churches holding fifty percent of the talents to create among them such a structure. Surely there is a pressing social need — finding vital pathways to assure the future and flourishing of the Episcopal Church as a compelling, international witness to the hope of the gospel — that is a common interest of the leaders of these parishes.

One thing needs to be confronted without cavil: It is not likely that our current institutional structures for decision-making and accountability — the General Convention, or the Executive Council — could to bring such a structure, or such a church, into being. This isn't a judgment on the capacity of these structures for adaptive change (which would seem to be inherently limited) so much as it is a linear assessment that relates the reasons these institutions were created to the objectives they have and the focus that orients their work.

The Church as Commonweal will be enabled to respond to God's call in mission by aligning the talents entrusted to a few with the possibilities of renewal and growth now emerging across the nine provinces and eighteen countries of our churches. When the church itself is seen as the focus of investment and nurturing, it will be enabled to find new paths toward serving and sending in Christ's name, and for adapting its message to speak incarnationally to a changing culture while staying true to its ethos.

Mark Edington is Bishop in charge of the Convocation of Episcopal Churches in Europe.

PART II

Church Profiles

❊ ❊ ❊

EIGHT

Christ Church Riverdale Builds on a 160-Year History

Christ Church Riverdale, Bronx, NY

Neva Rae Fox

Christ Church Riverdale in the Bronx experienced 13 percent growth from 2017 to 2021, and now it is adjusting to life after COVID. "There's no magic bullet for growth," said the Rev. Emily Anderson Lukanich, rector. "We experienced the growth from 2017, but with a change in leadership."Christ Church's strength, Lukanich said, is that the parish reflects its surrounding borough. "We are an incredibly diverse group. Multi-language is reflective of our community, and we look very much like our community."

Longtime parishioner Demitrio Acot agreed. "In a time of declining church participation and overall apathy, I believe we are sustaining and growing because we create real value for families and individuals. Our themes of diversity, welcoming without judgment or guilt, sense of family, and genuine support and care are just some of the reasons why people are proud to call Christ Church Riverdale their spiritual home." Acot added: "As a long-standing member of the Christ Church Riverdale choir, I believe we truly do our best to enhance the service and raise the worshiping experience of our fellow parishioners. The camaraderie throughout the years has been very important to me personally."

The parish also reflects diversity in age, Lukanich said, from the "very little ones to our oldest member who is 98." Christ Church sponsors a generation-spanning Sunday school because "churches are one of the last places where generations sit next to each other," Lukanich said. The parish has a strong history of 160 years. Its well-known parishioners included Mayor Fiorello La Guardia and the New York Yankees' legendary first baseman Lou Gehrig. Richard M. Upjohn was the architect of the Gothic Revival building, which was designated a New York City landmark[1] in 1966. "We are building on solid foundation," Lukanich said. "Christ Church has been an anchor in the community for many years." An AA group has met at the church for 80 years.

Christ Church, like most of society, is different post-pandemic. "We don't have as many bodies in the pews, but we have a lot of people online," Lukanich said. "The congregation is still engaged, but in different ways. We are connecting more organically, less programmatically." An inaugural post-lockdown step was to host small parties at

---

1   https://nylandmarks.org/site/christ-church-riverdale/

the rectory. "It's a mix of active members, newcomers, and some we haven't heard from in a while," Lukanich said. "It's a great way to get to know each other. Small parties allow people to connect." Among the congregational events that haven't changed are coffee hours and shared meals. "My people like to eat," Lukanich said, laughing.

A long-standing favorite tradition, halted during the pandemic, has returned — the international dinner. "We brought it back after pandemic," Lukanich said. "At the international dinner, everyone brings a dish from their country of origin. It's potluck, it's a small fundraiser. The parish hall is decorated with flags, and we invite community members." Christ Church maintains a long-standing relationship with Riverdale Community Center and neighboring churches for social ministry. It also works closely with the Northwest Bronx Clergy and Community Coalition. The church's ministries range from feeding people to teaching. Christ Church's food pantry "started with canned goods in a closet and now we do it once a week," Lukanich said. "We have a group that works with a school specifically for English-language students."

The church opens its doors and its "huge parish hall" to the community, she said. Arts groups, music programs, and children's theater are among those it welcomes. "We have music concerts four times a year, and that's the place where I see the community come back," Lukanich said. "We invite artists in. They know that when they come, they are welcome; when they call, we will help them. They might not know we are an Episcopal church." The goal, she explained, is "to reestablish our ties to the community. We can't always help the people across the world, but we can worry about the people closest to us that it affects."

"I think we are going through our challenges just like other parishes," Acot said. "It's not necessarily changes that have affected the church growth, but more of a sticking to our values, our commitment to our church, and — in effect — our commitment to each other."

Neva Rae Fox is a communications professional with extensive Episcopal experience, serving the boards of TLC Foundation, Bible and Common Prayer Book Society, Episcopal Community Services - NJ, and others.

NINE

St. John's Park Slope, Brooklyn: 'Just Getting Started'

St. John's, Brooklyn, NY

Neva Rae Fox

St. John's Park Slope describes itself as the second-oldest Episcopal church in Brooklyn, and adds: "But don't let our age fool you, we're just getting started." The Rev. Ben DeHart — a native of Princeton, New Jersey, who previously worked in Manhattan and Birmingham, Alabama — was called as rector more than a year ago. "Restarting churches is what we need to do," he said. Bishop Lawrence Provenzano of the Diocese of Long Island agreed: "Fr. Ben DeHart has come to St. John's with great enthusiasm, vision, and a working ecclesiology that fits perfectly into a renewed sense of mutual responsibility and inter-dependence within the congregation, the deanery, and the diocese."

DeHart looks at St. John's as a "198-year-old startup," and he says church attendance has been steadily rising. "We have more than doubled," he said. "It's been a great time."

St. John's location is a key to its growth," DeHart said. "Brooklyn is the borough of churches. We are showing people where they can be hooked in." The parishioners of St. John's mirror the diversity of Brooklyn, he said. "We talk about diversity, we talk about inclusion, but we mean it. This church reflects Brooklyn."

In addition to its multicultural members, St. John's boasts age diversity. "We have a decent amount of boomers, 20s, 30s, 40s," De-Hart said. "We are reflecting Brooklyn society." "Fr. DeHart's starting point, with this most diverse congregation, is built upon almost a decade of reconstruction and renovation, both to the physical plant and the spiritual life and focus of the people," Provenzano said. "This growth in ministry is an example of the cooperation and shared vision of the people of this diocese. The population of Brooklyn alone is almost 3 million people. The ministry field for our congregations is that population, not merely the people who attend liturgy on weekends. The right combination of liturgy, preaching, pastoral care, and teaching, along with care and action in the neighborhoods we serve, is growing the church in new and faithful ways."

While St. John's maintains customary church offerings like Bible study, altar guild, children's ministries, and music programs, it has developed two community-based options: summer hangs and an innovative hiking club. Both were born from congregants wanting to extend their camaraderie beyond Sunday mornings. "Most of the ministries happening at the church are likely expected for any congregation, but the hiking club is unique," said newer parishioner Micah

Goldston. The club began as the idea of a parishioner, and DeHart gave her "the freedom and space to organize and offer the outings to the congregation."

The summer hang began as a way to welcome DeHart. "One memory that continues to bubble up for me is the first of many Saturday barbecues in the courtyard this past summer, the rector's first summer at St. John's," Goldston said. "There, on a humid, sunny Saturday afternoon, surrounding a couple of tables, were individuals representing four generations — kids and teenagers, young adults, midlife adults and retirees — different ethnicities, and various socioeconomic backgrounds. Some people had been at the church for decades, others only a few Sundays. While no sacraments were offered, communion among believers was experienced that day."

DeHart believes in the power of social media. "I don't think social media is the end-all or be-all," he said, "but it's a start." St. John's maintains a presence on Instagram with 5,600 followers, and a Facebook page.

Texting is another strategic communications method. When newcomers visit, "we text or email that day," DeHart said. "It is great engagement. And the message is short and sweet: thank you for coming." Another growth element is branching out into the Park Slope area and broader Brooklyn. "We try to work in the community," DeHart said. The Park Slope Neighborhood Association meets at the church, and he connects with firefighters and community groups. "We get Park Slope people to come by."

Although he had not begun his ministry at St. John's during COVID, DeHart knows "the pandemic was not a great time for the church." One constructive change resulting from the lockdown was moving the Sunday service one hour earlier, to 10 a.m., which helped boost attendance. DeHart described St. John's as high church, which he considers an important point. "I really care about the preached word," DeHart said. "That exists to proclaim the good news of the gospel. Everything reflects the good news of the gospel."

Goldston agreed. "While there's nothing wrong with emphasizing social-justice matters within the church, I believe the rector's weekly emphasis on the 'Balm of Gilead' is a message that people need in their lives, and that's a large part of why people come back week after week."

DeHart admitted the Park Slope church has faced some issues. "We're a church that has been in the red for 20 years. There is no endowment, no back account. That has made the people of St John's more aware."

Like many churches, St. John's must address deferred maintenance. One current project is to rent the rectory as a revenue source. "We promised a balanced budget," he said. "We have to rent the rectory." DeHart has the confidence of his bishop, who added: "St. John's in Park Slope is an example of how faithfulness to a vision of 'the church being the church' focused on care for the wider community, ministry growth based on the sacramental and liturgical needs of God's people, preaching and living the gospel in real time, proper stewardship and use of buildings and other resources to support a vision for ministry grows the church."

TEN

Open Air Celebration

St. David's, Washington D.C.

Neva Rae Fox

The members of St. David's Church have stepped outside the parish's four walls and into the streets of a neighborhood of the nation's capital. With no lot and limited street parking, St. David's is "a neighborhood church" nestled in "one of the most expensive, pricey areas in D.C. to live in," said its rector, the Rev. Kristen L. Hawley. "We sit in the middle of a neighborhood that makes you feel like you are not in D.C." The Palisades neighborhood is about two and a half miles west of Washington National Cathedral.

She arrived in 2017 to a "small, faithful group championing the parish" after St. David's had been "downsizing for a decade." Since then, parochial reports indicate, St. David's has grown 35 percent from 2017 to 2021. "A huge part of it is going out and smiling and talking to everyone," Hawley said. "My gift is a lot of energy. I arrived with four kids, pregnant with number five." Hawley also credited storytelling, which "is fundamental for me. We told a new story of potential and new birth were possible. ... I am an abundance thinker. If you lead with abundance, you channel — you tell stories of — abundance. I helped people reclaim their stories."

Vestry member Rich Bland agreed with Hawley. "I believe her uncanny abilities in emphasizing family in all St. David's offerings, and her ability to share wonderful anecdotes in her sermons and pastoral ministry, have been the most significant factors, the secret sauce, if you will, for growth at St. David's." The first step was "letting the neighborhood know we were here," starting with outdoor movies, Hawley said. "Everyone in the community was welcome to come to the movies." A $10,000 grant from the Diocese of Washington helped cover projection equipment. The parish also moved all its coffee hours and St. Francis Day and Earth Day celebrations outside.

"When we hit COVID, we had already started to do things outside. Within six to eight weeks of the world shutting down, we were outside giving people a place to be that wasn't their house," Hawley said. "We leaned in and offered more during COVID that gave us a huge edge in growth. People wanted to worship." People wanted an opportunity to help during COVID, and St. David's gave them that opportunity. The neighborhood responded to drives for coats, gifts, and foodstuffs.

St. David's offered a chance for its neighbors to stand together on social concerns. "One particularly poignant memory of St. David's occurred in the aftermath of George Floyd's murder," vestry member Mary Kathryn Covert said. "The congregation gathered outside, as it was the height of COVID, and the church bells rang for nine minutes in reflecting the nine minutes Derek Chauvin was on George Floyd's neck. We all stood silently against this incredible injustice. We all stood for change. It was a powerful moment of community amongst so much divisiveness. That moment represented what we are — united against injustice, united together in faith and love." Now, St. David's is a community fixture "because we do everything outside; we're in the community all the time," Hawley said.

Initial growth came from families with young children, even among parents who not been churchgoers as they grew up. Bland said the emphasis on family helped the congregation's expansion. "Kristen Hawley has led unprecedented growth at St. David's by emphasizing family. Almost any event, service, or opportunity has an element that appeals to both children and parents, either together or separately. For those of us parents grappling with what it means to raise a child in the 21st century, this emphasis on the moral teachings of Christianity is like manna from heaven." He added, "Kristen also has a large family of her own. She is not afraid to share her own challenges and successes with raising her children. This also provides a much-needed humility and grace for us parishioners when we are anxiously looking for sources of wisdom."

Covert was drawn to St. David's through her children. "We have a 1-year-old and a 4-year-old, and they are always welcome, no matter the church event. We are in community with so many families, and it is this vibrancy as we walk in Christ's love that keeps us coming back." Now, Hawley reported, St. David's is welcoming "empty nesters, 50 to 70 years old, who are looking for a healthy, energized parish."

ELEVEN

'Loving the City' of Seguin, Texas

St. Andrew's, Seguin

Weston Curnow

An hour outside of San Antonio, nestled in beautiful Texas Hill Country, Seguin is a vibrant and growing community. Benefiting from the growth of the Sunbelt in recent years, Seguin's population has increased by over 16 percent in the last decade. At the center of this dynamic city stands St. Andrew's Episcopal Church. In the last three years, rector Stephen Shortess and the members of St. Andrew's have welcomed over 40 new members, a 13 percent increase in membership. Average Sunday attendance is up by more than 20 percent. "For us, it's all about community," said vestry member Susan Rinn.

"For us, COVID presented a moment to discern who and what we want to be," Shortess said. "It was then that we asked ourselves, 'How much can we mean to the people in our community?'" St. Andrew's transformed its church garden into a community garden, and began hosting nature walks. These changes attracted children and families, and became beloved features of the Seguin community.

St. Andrew's believes church should offer a fun family atmosphere. Christians "should not forget — the only way to keep tradition alive is to adapt," Shortess said.

Shortess said one of the most important aspects of emerging from the pandemic was making people "see how important we are for each other. ... And we do that by doing our best to love one another and rejoicing in the 5- and 95-year-old." St. Andrew's focuses its outreach on local matters. During the height of the pandemic, St. Andrew's started providing snacks for local nurses and forged a supportive relationship with Jefferson Elementary School.

Members of the church have also created a feeding ministry for students at Texas Lutheran University. On Sunday nights throughout the academic term, 20 to 30 parishioners feed more than 100 hungry college students. "It is our hope that when these students decide to look for a church home, they will remember the way the Episcopal Church treated them and cared for them," Shortess said. St. Andrew's works to be visible in the community through "a willingness to open the doors and be a part of it," Shortess said. "When we open our doors, we love this city. It is important for me to be out and about in our community." He added: "Enthusiasm is contagious. An enthusiastic rector makes for an inspired and responsive parish. Of course, this can only happen if there is a willingness and trust on behalf of the entire community."

Growth at St. Andrew's "has to do with who we are," Shortess said. "People feel very welcomed at St. Andrew's. People feel happy to be at St. Andrew's. People feel God's presence here. At St. Andrew's, we have a culture of welcome — everyone belongs." Shortess encourages other churches not to fear trying new approaches to ministry. "Be willing to take risks — what do we have to lose? God is always going to 'so love the world.' With that behind us, what do we have to fear?" For Shortess, Christians have all the reason to be the church in and of their communities — "God loves us so much, he is waiting at the doors of our church to go with us."

Weston Curnow is a student at the University of Kansas and assistant for liturgy and family ministries at St. Margaret's Church in Lawrence, Kansas.

TWELVE

Ted Lasso in Wales

St. Mary's, Brecon

Amber Noel

Call him Ted Lasso. Actually, call him Fr. Mark — unless you're a parishioner at St. Mary's Church in the hilly town of Brecon, Wales. A year ago, when a cheerful American priest, the Rev. Dr. Mark Clavier, became vicar of the small cathedral-town parish, St. Mary's had 16 regular Sunday worshipers. Today it has nearly 60, a growth rate of over 300 percent in a year, making for an underdog turnaround story like that of the football team on Apple TV's *Ted Lasso*. But how much does renewal reflect the new vicar's vibe? Though congregants speak very affectionately of their vicar's upbeat personality and people skills, there's a lot more than optimism behind the growth.

Clavier worked with the congregation early on to create a strategic plan, or a parish roadmap, called The Beacon Project. It integrates the small city's history with parishioners' stories. It asks questions like *Who are we? Where is God calling us to go? How will we get there?* It expresses the past, present, and hoped-for future of the congregation. You can pick up a Beacon Project booklet as soon as you walk in the door. The collaboration, clarity, and commitment of the document has created a sense of identity rooted in mission rather than survival or spiritual hospice care.

But part of this mission has meant treasuring a very traditional Anglican identity, even in a part of the world where growth usually means a more culturally evangelical style. St. Mary's history goes back to the Norman Conquest. A young couple, Kim Scally and Kris Lynch, have attended only a few months. "We felt very welcomed," Scally said. "It felt comforting." The first time they visited, they had just lost a son at 24 weeks' gestation. Looking for a sense of security and peace, they appreciated the familiarity of traditional worship and beauty of the historic space, combined with relational warmth.

"At a time when there was a lot of very raw grief and emotion," Lynch said, it was invaluable "to come to a place where we could heal and feel soothed, and feel the love of the Church." And the community is small enough that the couple already feels plugged in. Scally, an architect, is on the Beacon Project committee, helping plan improvements to the historic building. Renewal has also meant traditioned innovation, starting with their historical space. You can see this in St. Mary's cafe ministry. Parishioners turned the west end of the church, Monday to Saturday, into a restaurant and public meeting space. Parents meet for playdates and business partners have lunch in the side aisles, always within sight of the altar, and often hearing prayers or a Eucharist.

Though small, the church is high-ceilinged, creating a space that's airy, bright, and not overly intimate or closed in. Outside and inside flow together easily and naturally. The architecture lends a similar flexibility to the space, as might an all-purpose room in a nondenominational church, except instead of basketball hoops, St. Mary's visitors enjoy stained glass, a medieval Ting Tang bell, and stone soaked in centuries of prayer. The oldest definition of *parish* springs to mind.

Further reflecting St. Mary's discerned call to Benedictine hospitality and local rootedness, the Tower Cafe serves Brecon produce, bread, meat, and baked goods. Clavier leads midday services and hangs out in the cafe, where he finds many unplanned opportunities for ministry. In prayer, communal discernment, and strategic, missional risks, St. Mary's has opened outward in an organic way, welcoming the neighborhood to share a holy space and a shared inheritance.

Renewal has also meant investing in hours of prayer, budget adjustments, and building preservation. But the key to St. Mary's revival fits an even deeper lock. Clavier realized early on that to access the parish's history and inner life and cultivate growth would depend on learning from the handful of parishioners who'd weathered a precipitous decline. Faithful stewards of the church had stories to tell.

Dr. Elizabeth Parry — Liz to her church family — has been a parishioner for almost 25 years. Parry is a retired vicar's wife and a nurse. She and her husband came to St. Mary's looking for anonymity. When they came to the small, friendly church, they found "fantastic people." But "from day one," they did not feel like a diocesan priority.

"Pastoral care was minimal. I'm sure [the vicars] meant well, but the end result was that this felt like an orphan congregation."

In 2008, St. Mary's held a lay-led week of prayer in the Lady Chapel "to see where God was leading us." Parishioners sensed God's guidance, Parry said: "This is an ancient building, it has a Benedictine foundation, and our role was one of welcome and embracing." This dream lay fallow for many years as numbers fell, and some considered closing the parish permanently. "We have a lovely word in Welsh," Parry said. "It's *cwtch* [hug, cuddle]. My grandmother used to use it when she put the chickens away at night. You put the hens away in the *cwtch*. Safe. Warm. "It was a tragedy" waiting many years for a vicar to recognize "these are people who need loving," who need a *cwtch*.

Pillar members of St. Mary's could identify the vocations God had planted long ago in the DNA of the church, but to flourish, they first needed to feel loved. Committed plans for the future and a consistently hopeful attitude did more than cheer people up: it spoke directly to the congregation's particular wounds, communicated affection, and built trust.

Clavier knew this would be part of his job. But it also comes naturally. He simply loves Brecon — the town, the landscape, the Wye River. He and his wife, Sarah, love to hike in the hills with their dogs. They love the history of Wales. They love the local butcher. Vestry member Windsor Griffiths is a longtime parishioner, and he attributes renewed energy to having a priest who's obviously happy to be rooted in the parish, and who shares that with others: "people really want to work with him for the benefit of the Church's mission. The vibrancy in St. Mary's is beginning to infect more people in the area."

Liz Parry has seen qualitative change through the prayer ministry. There's been "a fundamental shift" in prayer requests, from focus on bereavement and grief to requests for guidance, from survival mode to being an active Christian presence in the community. "And if we as a church cannot meet people's needs, we need our bottoms slapped." Parry laughed, then added, "That's why we're here. We're the sanctuary. We're the ark. And we're building for the future."

A member since 2008, Jean Hosie felt the immediate difference it made for parishioners' pain to be acknowledged and their emotional needs met by what she called Clavier's "instant comprehension of the extremely negative and depressed situation he inherited." But she also saw the way the strategic plan made a baseline difference, not only to organizational challenges, but to the parish's mood: The "sense of a challenge to be met ... brought about an immediate reaction amongst long-standing and exhausted members, and at the same time attracted ... townspeople to find out what is going on."

A pastor's personality, like numbers, can probably be misread when looking at church growth. The vicar's vibe shouldn't drive growth or change. But personality and attitude undoubtedly have an influence. Affect has effect. It's worth wondering how our traits, moods, loves, and energy levels might be deployed for kingdom leadership. "Authenticity, being jovial, being traditional. St. Mary's is an example for me of how all these things can coexist," Kris Lynch said. "The Church can teach and preach the Word of God in the way it always has." But, said Kim Scally, "I wasn't anxious that I might slip up or be judged. I felt very accepted. That's what struck me."

So why is St. Mary's growing? Why was Ted Lasso's soccer team successful? "If I used one word, it would be community," Scally said.

"It's not just Sunday, it's every day of the week, and [it includes all] Brecon." Her husband added, "I look at the barbecue we had last weekend. It wasn't staged. It felt like a community." Like *Cwtch*? He smiled. "Yeah."

Amber D. Noel, M.Div., directs the public-facing programs of The Living Church, *including the podcast, events, and the Partner program. Outside of work, she is a writer and enjoys life in Atlanta.*

THIRTEEN

Renewed Fellowship, New Staff Bring Growth

Trinity Church Cathedral, Columbia, SC

Bonnie N. Scott

When the Very Rev. Dane Boston returned to Trinity Cathedral in Columbia, South Carolina, this time as dean in January 2021, he found a very different church than the one he had previously served as canon for adult formation for five years. "My first Sunday at the cathedral, which seats 700 people, I looked out at 70 because that's what the pandemic-safe seating permitted," Boston said. After serving as rector of Christ Church in Cooperstown, New York, he was called back to Trinity. Even as one of the largest Episcopal churches in the area, it was struggling to adapt to the new pandemic reality.

Just as many churches did, Trinity began livestreaming services and adapted to a socially distanced world. While church life was largely diminished as a result, for some parishioners, especially older legacy members of Trinity, this was a blessing that could not have been predicted. "The technology has allowed many to reconnect with the community," Boston said. "A 90-year-old parishioner told me that she felt more connected with Trinity through the pandemic than she had for a decade."

Dane Boston offers a blessing during an Ash Wednesday service. In the two years since Boston's return, and with the ebbing of pandemic restrictions, Trinity has seen remarkable growth. The church has boasted a 29 percent increase in average Sunday attendance, from 779 in 2017 to 1,004 in 2021. The growth rate is especially impressive because the church was starting from much larger than the usual size for Episcopal churches. "I think as we've come back, there is a new sense of how much we all need one another. There's a real desire to re-establish relationships and share in fellowship with one another," Boston said. While previously ministries were somewhat siloed from one another, resulting in uneven participation, Boston says that the congregation has come together in new ways that he could not have predicted.

During the Feast of the Epiphany service this year, 12 new members were inducted into the boys' choir — a remarkable number compared to past years. Previously at Trinity, there had been an oyster roast after the service, separate and apart from the service and with different participants. This year, everyone spilled from the church onto the lawn together, a clear sign of a newfound fellowship the congregation has been experiencing.

According to Boston, Trinity has seen growth from new parishioners who were not previously connected to the Episcopal Church. This year, this category made up the majority of Trinity's new confirmands. Trinity has also seen a revitalization of multigenerational families attending services together which, even before the pandemic, had been in slight decline.

And what is drawing people to Trinity? Boston attributes the growth to many factors, some of which are non-replicable. Trinity is the large, downtown cathedral in Columbia, so for many people who are looking for a church, the cathedral is the first stop. It also shares a historical connection with Heathwood Hall Episcopal School, which has served as a pipeline to Trinity for some families connected to the school. But Boston attributes a significant degree of Trinity's growth to its popular music program and new investments in ministries for families. While there had been some staff turnover, Trinity recently hired a full-time director of children and family ministries for a position that had historically been part time.

"God has given me people right when we needed it," Boston said. "The vestry was very supportive of this being the moment to invest in the community, and I think we're seeing a huge response from the congregation as a result." In an age in which technology and social isolation have exacerbated feelings of loneliness and disconnection for many parishioners across congregations, Boston finds opportunities for fellowship critical. "I think at this time in our culture and in our church, gathering people together doesn't have to have an agenda or programmatic element," he said. "Just being together is so important."

While some may criticize non-programmatic gatherings lacking an emphasis on worship, Boston thinks these events are ripe with the opportunity for formation and a necessary part of a healthy, thriving church community. "While I take these criticisms seriously, I think even these kinds of social gatherings can ultimately draw people deeper into lives of faith," he said. "This is a season in which we first have to regather our strength as a community and rebuild those bonds so that we can go deeper theologically and pursue our ministries."

Boston says Trinity's growth has not been the result of a carefully executed master plan, but rather has emerged from a talented and faithful staff, helped by a great deal of luck. "We have been blessed at a particular moment and a particular time," Boston said. "All glory be to God!"

Bonnie N. Scott, M.Div., is an editor for The Living Church *and currently resides in New Orleans with her husband and daughter.*

FOURTEEN

Spreading the Welcome Mat in Hill Country

St. Michael and All Angels, Blanco, TX

Mike Patterson

When David and Taylor Smith pushed a baby stroller along the quiet streets of their neighborhood in Blanco, Texas, the walks took them past St. Michael and All Angels Episcopal Church, a couple of blocks away and around the corner from their home along the Blanco River. Friends next door "told us how great the church was" and invited them to attend a service. "We loved how the members of the church, prior to a service, engaged with one another," David Smith said. "We loved the idea of a tight-knit church family, so we chose to go to St. Michael's. We immediately felt at home due to the kindness and sense of community within the body."

The Smiths are among many new members who have joined St. Michael's in the last few years. The mission of the church is to make them "feel welcome and wanted," said the Rev. Bryn Caddell, St. Michael's vicar. "They are looking for connection, and we're offering a place for them to connect." "The church family has been wonderfully gracious, kind, and inviting of our young family," Taylor Smith added. "We wanted our children, both under the age of 4, to know that their church family was there to guide them, watch over them, and love on them. We found that at St. Michael's."

According to its annual parochial reports, St. Michael's has seen a 45.9 percent increase in average Sunday attendance between 2017 and 2022. This translates into an increase from 37 people on an average Sunday to 54 in 2022. The Sunday attendance in 2023 is already averaging nearly 26 percent above 2022. Membership has likewise jumped 32.8 percent, to 89 members from 67, and plate and pledge offerings have risen from $65, 977 in 2017 to $121,045 in 2022 — a whopping 83.4 percent increase in five years.

"Growth did not come as a surprise, but the amount of growth has been surprising," said Bishop's Warden Bubba Groos, who married his wife, Carol, at St. Michael's in 1998. They joined the church in 1997 and are among the longest-attending members. Founded as a mission of the Diocese of West Texas in 1953, St. Michael's has throughout much of its history maintained an average attendance of 30 to 40. Its recent spurt of growth places it closer to pastoral-sized churches in the diocese.

"In our diocese of 85 missions and parishes, we are larger than 53 of them," Caddell said. "We are trying to learn how to transition from being a family-sized church to being a pastoral-sized church. That means that the whole church doesn't necessarily need to weigh in to decide which shrub to plant or what type of lawnmower to buy, and that is an adjustment. These aren't downsides at all, but they are growing pains." For most of its history, St. Michael's was served by a vicar whose role was to offer Holy Communion on Sunday and conduct the occasional wedding or funeral. When Caddell graduated from the Seminary of the Southwest during the COVID-19 pandemic in 2020, Bishop David M. Reed assigned her to serve as a part-time deacon at St. Michael's because it was already experiencing some growth. She was ordained a priest in December 2020.

"The hope was that with a part-time priest, the congregation would continue to grow enough to justify a full-time position," Caddell said. That goal was achieved in July 2022 with financial support from the diocese. "Full-time clergy translates into more pastoral care, more interaction with the community, and more programs being offered, which all can help promote growth," she said. "I certainly hoped that the congregation would grow. In light of the pandemic, the rate of growth has been a surprise."

Located in a semi-rural area in the heart of the Texas Hill Country, 50 miles north of San Antonio and 54 miles west of Austin, Blanco and neighboring communities are growing at a faster rate than Texas as a whole "due to people moving here upon retirement and, to a lesser extent, the increase in a remote working culture that allows people to work from a more peaceful environment," Groos said. Some parishioners drive about 30 miles one way to attend services. "The pandemic taught people that they didn't necessarily need to live close to an office in a big city," Caddell said. "Blanco is attractive to people who want to move from the city and enjoy wide open spaces."

"Our main strategy has simply been to welcome people who visit," she added. "Folks moving to a small town know that church is a great place to meet people. They are looking to make friends and get involved in the community." Those joining St. Michael's are a mixture of adults from several generations — baby boomers, Gen Xers and millennials, Groos said. They include a range of retirees and young families like the Smiths, with children ranging from infants to high school and college-age students. Groos said a substantial part of St. Michael's growth has been the addition of a couple of intergenerational family clusters. "It seems that if some people in our community come and like it, they attract more of their family," he said. "We have other members that are bringing friends to visit."

Groos credited Caddell with launching "programs that just weren't feasible without someone having a full-time impact." For example, she has trained youth for service at the altar and instituted a Youth Sunday when youth serve as acolytes, hosts, Eucharistic ministers, oblation-bearers, and lectors. She has also started midweek and Sunday Bible studies, as well as a weekly fellowship hour for church members over Zoom. Many of the new members already have an affiliation with the Episcopal Church when they move to the area, Groos said. David Smith was baptized at an Episcopal church in San Antonio but was primarily raised a Baptist. His wife, Taylor, was raised at Christ Church in Plano, north of Dallas, when it was an Episcopal church.

"Certainly, there are the Episcopalians — people who have moved to Blanco and had been active members of Episcopal churches in Austin, Houston, San Antonio, and elsewhere," Caddell said. "They are excited about plugging in and joining our altar guild or becoming lay readers. They also bring with them best practices from other churches and have been helpful in offering suggestions about new things we could try or consider. "There are also visitors who weren't Episcopalians before, but simply visited the churches in town and found a home with us.

"Because we are growing, a good percentage of our church have been members for less than five years. I think it feels more comfortable to be new in a place where there are lots of other people who were new not that long ago. They can share experiences and stories about moving, building houses, and making their way in a new community." Groos said St. Michael's makes it a point to offer a "welcoming fellowship" to visitors. "A number of our newer members have mentioned that what attracted them to our church is the fact that they were welcomed so warmly," he said.

Visitors are given welcome bags and are greeted by many members. Everyone is encouraged to wear nametags to help both new and longtime members get to know each other. Caddell sends a monthly newsletter and weekly update to keep church members informed. And a new feature called "Meet Our Members" has been added to help introduce parishioners to each other. Caddell is "keenly attuned to the meeting and greeting" of visitors, Groos said. It is important to meet with new members and "have a conversation about how they would like to be involved," Caddell said.

To help make newcomers feel more welcome and part of the church family, St. Michael's started holding an annual newcomers dinner to invite new members to meet and socialize with the Bishop's Committee and the vicar. The church is now planning semi-annual dinners to accommodate the growth in membership.

Another way St. Michael's has introduced visitors and members to the church is by continuing its long tradition of potluck luncheons after services on the first Sunday of each month. "A potluck is an easy way to invite participation," Caddell said. "Everyone can contribute. And there is nothing better than to have a reason and opportunity to sit down and get to know the people with whom you worship. Once someone feels known, and knows others in return, they tend to stay. They become part of the church because they are in relationship with the people."

With growth has come "a palpable change in the vibrancy of the fellowship," Groos said. "There is also the energy and sound of toddlers, which is joyful to most of our members." But with growth has come pressing management issues, especially concerning possible solutions to capacity issues, such as the addition of worship services or other overflow solutions. He called this a "fortunate problem." The COVID-19 pandemic changed some things immediately, such as initial remote worship requirements, Groos said. "But in addition, it prompted a quick advance of more technological changes that have been beneficial post-pandemic," he said. "Our worship is available on-line, along with remote giving via our website. The ability to do this has enabled expansion of in-person worship so that our parish hall can be used for overflow on crowded Sundays."

"The pandemic has been part of my ordained ministry from the start," Caddell said. "St. Michael's was originally livestreaming using Zoom. We transitioned to YouTube and have continued to livestream our services. "In order to allow for socially distanced seating, we used the adjacent parish hall for overflow space. Fortunately, we already had the technology for that. There was a television in the parish hall that had been used from time to time for large funerals. We haven't stopped using the parish hall, but now, instead of socially distanced seating, it is regularly used as worship space and includes a children's area."

While the church seats about 60, "it is possible to squeeze more in, but people generally self-select to move into the parish hall rather than pack in tight with one another," Caddell said. As of May 7, the average Sunday attendance was 68, compared to a 2020 pre-pandemic ASA of 46. "We regularly have people in our overflow area in the parish hall," she said. "When we have more than 80 people, which has happened a handful of times already, our overflow area starts to fill up as well." This has led to conversations about moving from one service on Sunday to two services, perhaps starting as early as this fall.

Asked for his advice on connecting with new people, Groos replied: "Throw out the welcome mat! Encourage your parishioners to make it a point to personally meet visitors and introduce themselves, and make sure your clergy do the same." He added: "Broaden methods of communication via inclusion in churchwide email distributions and an online presence where visitors can find your church and know when services and events are being held, and have access remotely to worship to get a 'feel' for what your church is like."

"Engage the Holy Spirit, and come up with a reason to invite people," Caddell said. Since St. Michael is one patron saint of first responders and warriors, "we held a St. Michael's Day celebration in 2021 and invited our neighbors and city officials to participate in a blessing of first responders and veterans. It was a way to let our community know who we are, what we value, and what we do. St. Michael's Day in 2022 was a bigger event than the first one, and we're already starting to make plans for 2023."

David Smith said that "the actions of our church were attractive: a commitment to love their neighbors, show love through kindness and fostered an atmosphere of Christlikeness in how they treat one another as family." "The Holy Spirit is at work here," Caddell said. "People are looking for a connection with the holy, and they are finding it in this community."

Mike Patterson is a freelance writer based in San Antonio and a member of St. Michael's.

FIFTEEN

What is Jesus Doing Right Now?

St. Anne's Church, Middletown, DE

Dylan Thayer

At St. Anne's Episcopal Church in Middletown, Delaware, cultivating a mindset of growth and openness to the community is a matter of presentation and routine. "You get up in the morning, you shower, you shave, you put on clean clothes," says the Rev. Russell Bohner, TSSF, who has served as the parish's rector since 2014. "You look sharp."

Just as we have these morning rituals and try to make ourselves look presentable before leaving the house, Bohner says, parishes need to put on their best possible image for newcomers experiencing their church — or any church — for the first time. In Bohner's view, this includes making sure the building and grounds are "vibrant, alive, and inviting" — no peeling paint or dismal bathrooms — and extends to virtual spaces, such as the website and hybrid worship, a must for any church in the post-pandemic era.

But while what's on the outside is important, Bohner stresses that what's within sets St. Anne's apart. Bohner is a cradle Episcopalian who grew up in the First State, and he's spent all 11 of his years in ordained ministry in Delaware. So perhaps he's a bit biased when he assesses St. Anne's as a "small congregation with a good heart and a good core" and considers the church's friendliness fundamental to its growth during the past nine years. But the results speak for themselves: according to Bohner, St. Anne's average Sunday attendance has grown from around 105 in 2014 to 160 in March of 2020, just before the pandemic began.

"The people, when I arrived, were eager to be church," Bohner says, and joy has become the primary ingredient in everything the congregation does. "Joy is an overlooked gift of the Holy Spirit. ... We're here [on Sunday mornings] to celebrate." Music and liturgy are important to St. Anne's, but embracing the movement of the Spirit in sometimes unexpected ways is even more essential. "It's OK that the baby's crying," Bohner says. "It's OK that the liturgy wasn't perfect. Let's live into freedom. Doesn't mean that anything goes, but let's not be obsessive about this."

As an example of this attitude, Bohner relates the story of a little girl who was hanging out in the aisle while he was preparing to celebrate the Lord's Supper. Bohner invited her up to the altar with him, and now the children of St. Anne's routinely congregate there during the Eucharist. The children around the altar reflect the diverse group of people flocking to the congregation. Again, Bohner believes that the liturgy and music are attractive, and he's quick to heap praise on the parish's music minister, whose repertoire ranges from traditional Anglican hymns to gospel music. This mix of innovative and familiar music has been warmly received by new and old faces alike.

But Bohner believes the emphasis on a Sunday-morning experience that borders on the provocatively countercultural and remains deeply faithful to the gospel message is the biggest reason why people of so many different backgrounds — young, old, gay, straight, Black, white, conservative, liberal — all find a home at St. Anne's. Bohner is blunt and moving on his primary responsibility as a preacher and pastor: "I don't care if you're a good Democrat, I don't care if you're a good Republican. I'm here to invite you into a totally different way of living in the world: to be genuinely Christian, and have that be your primary identity. If we're really preaching the gospel, it will have something to aggravate everyone. Our identity in Christ does not have any other category. It does not fit neatly into preexisting categories."

Above all, Bohner believes that people don't come to church to experience fellowship, music, preaching, or anything else but Christ himself. He tells each newcomer leaving St. Anne's for the first time: "I hope you experienced God here this morning." And Bohner is thrilled by the number of people who say yes, and the energy and enthusiasm he sees building at St. Anne's. "People are excited to join us because we're doing what we love," he says. "It's not 'What would Jesus do?' It's 'What is Jesus doing right now?'"

A lifelong Episcopalian, Dylan Thayer is a contributing writer.

SIXTEEN

Not Defined
by a Building
(Or Lack Thereof)

St. Mary's, Hillsboro, TX

Christine Havens

In discussing their parish, Roberta and David Skelton remember the laughter of the Rev. Hunter Ruffin, one of the priests who has helped them in recent years. They offer a simple description of those attracted to St. Mary's Episcopal Church in Hillsboro, Texas: "Happy people." This phrase came not just from the Skeltons but also from other members, who took time during one of their Lenten Soup suppers to discuss their church.

This seems to be St. Mary's personality as a whole — an infectious buoyancy combined with resilience and a determination to be instruments of God's grace despite losing their worship space twice in the church's 150-year history. The first time occurred in 1894, after a tornado destroyed the first church building.

For a while after that, as a 150th anniversary history relates, "services were again held in Sarah Margaret Sturgis' parlor," where St. Mary's began in 1872. She started Sunday school classes there, and services were soon added, followed by a church building in 1886. After the tornado, the congregation worshiped in a temporary space until 1911, when a new building was completed.

The second loss was much more intimate and more painful, but is nonetheless an integral part of St. Mary's current growth. In 2008, when most churches in the Episcopal Diocese of Fort Worth left to join the Anglican Church of North America (ACNA), St. Mary's members were divided. As the church's history notes, "for the next twelve years, St. Mary's was the only church in the embattled diocese to share space with the other side. We shared space: Episcopalians had their service at eleven o'clock, while the other group had an earlier service. We shared flowers at Easter and Christmas."

At the conclusion of lengthy litigation, ownership of their shared space was awarded to the ACNA congregation, now known as St. Mary's Anglican Church. St. Mary's Episcopal Church was uprooted again, and after 110 years, members are again in a temporary building — a former drive-through bank located near the center of Hillsboro, about an hour south of Ft. Worth. This experience is akin to becoming a forced church plant, with the temptation to become stunted and bitter. Instead, St. Mary's is growing and asking what new opportunities God might be opening up.

In the last three years, the congregation has doubled from 11 members to 23, which parishioners said came as a complete surprise. In addition to the split, St. Mary's experienced the normal attrition from members dying or moving away. However, the pandemic led to one new member, and family connections have helped attract others. The man who became St. Mary's junior warden was motivated by his sister-in-law to watch online services from an Episcopal church near Houston. He had not been active in a church before then. Once in-person worship was available again, he searched online for a local church and both St. Mary's appeared on his computer's screen.

After a phone conversation about the differences between Episcopal and ACNA beliefs, he chose to visit and has not missed a Sunday since. Other new members include relatives who moved to Hillsboro or who already lived in the area and saw how much their wife or mother enjoyed fellowship and they joined. New members have meant a baptism this year, a blessing of a same-sex marriage, and a confirmation service in April.

St. Mary's is a lay-led congregation for now. David Skelton has been the bishop's warden essentially since the congregation divided. Junior Warden John Fitch doubles as treasurer. Their wives serve as the altar guild with occasional help. Most of the congregation's families are represented on the Bishop's Committee, but they make most decisions by consensus of the congregation.

The church's music director, Sandi Farmer, leads Bible study before services. St. Mary's also has an active Daughters of the King chapter. When they don't have a priest, they read Morning Prayer and members sign up to read the lessons or the sermon (from *Sermons That Work*). Many supply priests have served this small, hardy congregation. Supply priests have helped the church for 14 years. At one point after the division, St. Mary's had one priest in charge for about six months.

"She was marvelous but was called away by the Seminary of the Southwest," Skelton said. The Rev. Hope Benko, who is now the seminary's vice president of enrollment, calls St. Mary's "committed and loving." Fr. Hunter Ruffin, of the fondly remembered laugh, supplied there often and thinks highly of the people he encountered. He is not surprised that they're growing. The congregation attributes much of St. Mary's growth not only to being located on a main street of town and recently putting up a large sign, but also to being very active in the community, both corporately and individually. They are too small to administer a new, area-wide program, but they help with a variety of community services.

Most significantly, the church has given away 40 percent of its offerings since 2009. That doesn't take into account the time and talent it has given. Members partner with area churches and other entities, including Hill County Kids, which provides weekend food packs for children receiving free breakfast and lunches through schools, and the Hillsboro Interfaith Ministry food pantry, which feeds about 600 families a month.

What was, briefly, the Diocese of North Texas has reunited with the Diocese of Texas, and it's too soon to know what effect that may have on St Mary's growth. Members are hopeful, as the Diocese of Texas "has abundant resources and opportunities," David Skelton says. "We are trying to find how to find a plate at the table."

In the meantime, the underlying factor in St. Mary's growth is simply its members' faith in God. "We are the church," the history of St. Mary's says. "The church is wherever we are, just as God is with us wherever we are. In good times and in bad, through tornadoes and human-made destruction, the church, St. Mary's Episcopal Church, continues to celebrate God's love and to be Christ's voice, hands, and feet in the world today."

Christine Havens is a writer and a graduate of the Seminary of the Southwest. She is passionate about literature and theology. Her work has appeared on Mockingbird Ministries' blog, Mbird, *and in* Soul by Southwest, *the seminary's literary journal.*

SEVENTEEN

Looking for Partners Helps Illinois Parish Grow

St. Luke's Episcopal Church, Evanston, IL

Bonnie N. Scott

The Rev. Kat Banakis, rector of St. Luke's Episcopal Church in Evanston, knows her church is well-positioned for growth. Nestled in the northern Chicago suburb, the home of Northwestern University and a city frequently listed as popular among retirees, St. Luke's benefits greatly from a steady stream of newcomers of all ages. The population growth of Evanston, however, does nothing to diminish the surprising successes at St. Luke's in the past three years, when so many churches have seen steep declines in numbers. In 2019, when Banakis became rector, St. Luke's had an average Sunday attendance of 155. It grew to

170 in 2020 and 173 in 2021, an 11.6 percent increase in three years.

When the pandemic began, Banakis had only been serving the congregation for nine months, and she and St. Luke's leadership pivoted to the new reality her congregation faced. "Phone buddies" were established to keep congregants connected and checking in on one another. New ministries such as book clubs and adult formation groups were established online. They have since moved to hybrid models, allowing for a broader reach. "Continuing online worship and moving educational programs online, throughout the pandemic and since, allowed for a far broader reach in terms of formation than we ever thought possible," Banakis said.

Banakis attributes some of St. Luke's growth to a renewed focus on justice initiatives and partnerships with other congregations. Since the summer of 2020, St. Luke's has worked with other houses of worship on projects such as Sacred Ground, an Episcopal film-based dialogue series on race and faith, as well as reparations in Evanston.

"We partnered with 16 other historically white houses of worship from across Evanston in order to make a contribution and a statement about reparations," Banakis said. "We looked into our racial history as a congregation and shifted our focus to social-justice ministry as a major pillar. This has allowed us to work with the interfaith community in Evanston, which was already quite strong. This has definitely expanded our reach as a church."

St. Luke's partnerships have also focused on children's and young-adult ministry within the Episcopal Church. "Being intentional in our partnering has allowed all of us to offer more than any of us could do on our own," Banakis said. A confirmation class held with other local Episcopal churches had 15 participants, rather than St. Luke's normal three or four. With its congregational growth, St. Luke's has hired a new children's minister. Banakis believes this increases St. Luke's demographic reach and makes it a more attractive church for families with young children. "When you have new families coming in, you have to keep finding new ways of getting them engaged," Banakis said. Eighty percent of St. Luke's congregants participate in some form of its ministries in addition to worship.

Since St. Luke's has experienced large growth on both ends of the age spectrum — young families and senior citizens — this requires programming that speaks to each group. These ministries are not static, but constantly growing and expanding to meet the needs of community and the interests of the congregation, a change Banakis attributes in part to the flexibility and quick changes demanded by the pandemic. One such change was participating in a multi-congregation initiative to house the homeless in churches during the coldest winter months. While St. Luke's had not participated in the past, with services and programs online during 2020, it has opened the parish doors for the last two years, with no plans of stopping.

"Now when people come in the doors, what they're hearing and seeing in the bulletin announcements is beautiful music, preaching, and lived theology, but also an intentional focus on interfaith social-justice work," Banakis said. "In any congregation, this can often be a small, cellular unit, but when you're looking at citywide initiative, there is so much more that can be done."

Banakis sees long-term benefits to interfaith, community-based work. "As we look at the future of the church, there's going to be denominational shift and change," she said. "An important responsibility for faith leaders is to prepare congregations for that. What can we do now to be partnering with other congregations in our communities? It's important that we can embrace these changes now so that we're really ready for these shifts down the line." In many ways, Banakis said, St. Luke's has already asked many of these difficult questions, and this preparatory work has led the parish to where it is today. In the early 2000s, the congregation dwindled to a fraction of its former size and began serious conversations about its future.

After deciding to remain open, St. Luke's slowly built back, and then experienced the growth it has seen in the last three years. St. Luke's story of renewal offers a hopeful vision of what remains possible for congregations struggling with declining numbers. What advice does Banakis have for other congregations? "Being honest about the demographics in your area and what growth is possible within your context is important. I also think playing to the strengths of your already existing congregation is essential. For us, partnering with other churches has really been life-giving and energizing in a way that we never could have done alone."

EIGHTEEN

Waxing the Surfboard at Holy Trinity, West Palm Beach

Holy Trinity, West Palm Beach, FL

Dylan Thayer

The Rev. Rutger-Jan (R-J) Heijmen — rector of Holy Trinity, West Palm Beach, Florida — talks a lot about water, appropriately enough for a man whose congregation is a few miles west of the Atlantic Ocean. "All ministry is waxing the surfboard and waiting for God to send the waves," he says. The past three years of coronavirus have been filled with waves for Heijmen and for Holy Trinity. But God's waves have nevertheless brought opportunities for him and his church, whose average Sunday attendance has grown by over 30 percent since 2019. When Heijmen arrived at Holy Trinity in January 2020, he appreciated the church's strong culture — Heijmen repeatedly mentions his gratitude that the parish called him — yet was determined to make his mark.

"I'm not afraid to take risks," he also repeats, and his résumé proves it. Heijmen has a highly entrepreneurial outlook on ministry, honed during many years of evangelistic outreach to youth and young adults and his role in planting a church in New York City. But when the COVID-19 pandemic began, the waves only grew higher. Before accepting the call to Holy Trinity, Heijmen served at St. Martin's in Houston for seven years. Heijmen and his family decided that he would commute between West Palm Beach and Houston while his son finished his senior year of high school. After flights were grounded in March 2020, Heijmen remained in Houston for months, and had to shepherd his congregation through Lent, Easter, and beyond from hundreds of miles away.

In Houston, Heijmen produced as much digital content as he could, including not just the typical Coronatide fare of Zoom fellowship, worship, and ministries, but also YouTube daily devotionals for Lent, and sermons interspersed with clips from popular movies and TV shows. Holy Trinity's vestry members and other laity were instrumental during Heijmen's absence, creating a phone tree that ensured every parishioner remained connected to the broader congregation. "Our congregation was determined to do everything they could to stay in touch with each other," Heijmen said.

Holy Trinity relaunched in-person worship in October 2020. Despite his comfort with digital media and the parish's continued reliance on it — "streaming is going to be here forever," Heijmen says, adding that more than 100 people still participate online each Sunday — Holy Trinity remained "determined to bring everyone back together as soon as possible." Again, Heijmen and his congregation were not afraid to do something bold and innovative to make it happen. "Our vestry worked courageously during this time," Heijmen said, especially in launching an outdoor ministry in early 2021, which began as "Lent in a Tent" but lasted far beyond that liturgical season.

At first it looked as though Lent in a Tent might not launch. Heijmen awoke multiple times during the night before the first service, startled by a huge storm that drenched and battered West Palm Beach. But come morning, the tent was still standing, along with 80 worshipers, many of them new to both Holy Trinity and the Episcopal Church."Our parishioners were really excited about what we were doing, and that energy fed on itself, and they did a great job of inviting their friends, family, anyone they could think of, to church," Heijmen says. By June, the outdoor service had grown to more than 300. Many of the newcomers told Heijmen and others that they had never enjoyed church so much and that worship at Holy Trinity was the highlight of their week.

Heijmen credits Holy Trinity's inclusive culture, diverse congregation, and relatively casual worship setting for this atmosphere. "You can truly be yourself at Holy Trinity," he says. That attitude extends to political identity. "We are not here to be Fox News or MSNBC," Heijmen says. "We are here to talk about eternal things, and we are here to talk about your things." Heijmen believes the gospel demands our votes as well as our hearts. But he worries that being too political can distract from a Christian's true focus: Christ.

Heijmen has not always thought this way, but he now appreciates that his younger, more politically vociferous self "did not change any minds or any hearts. It only hardened people who did not agree with me and emboldened those who did. I try to ask people to draw their hearts closer to Jesus, and let the Holy Spirit do the rest. When people draw near to Jesus, their hearts begin to change, almost in spite of themselves." It is a recurring theme, and one Heijmen emphasizes when asked about how churches can better help their neighbors. Heijmen is full of pragmatic solutions: keep the service to a reasonable length, make sure the bulletin is newcomer-friendly, be missional in your outlook, make sure the rector has a good therapist, and do not be afraid to take risks.

Waxing the surfboard takes a lot of time and energy. But Heijmen is also clear on who moves the waves. "People really want to know about Jesus. That is why they are here," he said. "Preach God's mercy, grace, love, forgiveness for broken people who don't deserve it. Teach the Bible as much as possible. People want to know what's in there."

NINETEEN

Progress in the Pandemic: Christ Church, Tulsa

Christ Church, Tulsa, TX

William Hargrave

When the Rev. Everett Lees assumed the role of Christ Church's rector in 2011, the average Sunday attendance (ASA) was about 40. Years later, just before the pandemic, Christ Church[1] was identified as one of the fastest-growing Episcopal parishes in the country, with a 2018 ASA of 207, and 230 for 2019. Tulsa's population grew by only half of one percent between 2013 and 2018, according to the World Population Report, while Christ Church's ASA grew by 93 percent.

Lees says that one of the defining moments in the life of the par-

---

1   *Christ Church, Tulsa, is a partner of* The Living Church.

ish was when parishioners collectively shifted their priority from trying to do everything to doing just a few things really well. This attitude particularly benefited Christ Church in the pandemic, when, rather than busying himself and the church staff with increasing their online presence, Lees worked to meet his congregation's other needs. "There's no need to do what others are already doing well, and it's important to be totally okay with that" he said. "There are already Daily Office podcasts. You can really just sit there and say, 'Hey, Alexa, pray Morning Prayer.'"

So instead, Lees focused the parish's efforts on community building. "Pre-COVID, we thought of community as the service we attend. While this isn't bad, what it told us was that we need to have connecting points other than the Sunday morning worship." As a result, Christ Church has been organizing small groups based on the study of Scripture and a custom curriculum adapted from a sermon series from Alpha. After recognizing that there was a growing number of families in the area, the church "made some intentional decisions to really build children's programming," Lees told *TLC* last year. "We were fortunate in that we had some folks who had some experience with Godly Play, and we were able to implement that."

The church also hired a children's minister, "before we even had a lot of kids," he said. "We jumped out in a leap of faith, and we built something for the congregation we hoped to become." It has paid off — up to a third of current attendance is kids fifth grade and below. The current ASA is about 140. In addition to offering outdoor services for the last year, Christ Church has also been arranging concerts for local musicians as an opportunity for members of the community to simply come together again. The church also supports opportunities to give blood, and volunteers pack meals for those who were displaced during the pandemic. "What are people wanting post-COVID? That sense of community that pandemic exposed such a deep hunger for," Lees said.

Christ Church's summer programs include a spiritual retreat focused on liturgical and contemplative prayer, and classes on the fundamentals of the Christian faith and the Anglican church, all free and available to anyone who is interested. Christ Church's Facebook page lists one frequently asked question: What if I can't attend all the sessions? "It is ok if you can't attend all sessions, the week you miss will likely cover the secrets of life."

William Hargrave is a graduate of the University of the South (Sewanee).

PART III

Practical Wisdom

❋ ❋ ❋

TWENTY

A Manifesto for Daily Offices

Clint Wilson

I have heard it said the monks of Mt. Athos, whose daily existence and lives are surrounded by the waters of the mighty Mediterranean Sea, understand their vocations, which spring forth from prayer, as releasing an intense concentration of the blazing warmth of God's love as it spills outward and hovers over the waters and abroad to all the world. Similarly, I envision my parish chapel being a furnace of faith, spilling out the *heat* of prayer, providing the warmth of God's love and presence to our surrounding community, often amid tumultuous and trying times in which people feel as though they are drowning in the waters. I know, I am a romantic.

Until recently, however, the chapel, just off of our Nave, has remained largely under-utilized, except for two liturgies and a children's chapel service on Sunday (all of which are wonderful). During the week it sits empty, like a fireplace without a fire, and I have longed for it to pulsate with the heat of God's presence of prayer working through his people. For this reason, among others, my parish is committing to praying the daily offices of Morning and Evening Prayer starting this Lent and lasting, I hope, until the kingdom comes.

WHY WOULD WE DO THIS?

Anglicans have always thought it not only salutary but necessary to breathe with *both* lungs of the spiritual life — the Bible and prayer — which are brought together in harmony in the daily offices. If our conversion extends throughout our lives, which I find to be tacitly true (we *are* saved on the cross, we are *being* saved, and we *will be* saved on the last day), then our imaginations and desires must be converted as well, and this happens through saturation in sacred Scripture and attentiveness to the grace of God and his gospel, unearned and unmerited.

To be sure, there are many expressions, gifts, and practices related to the entire body, as Paul uses the metaphor in 1 Corinthians 12, which are important for the church *to be* the church. However, these are all utterly dependent upon and governed by our encounter with God through Scripture and prayer (including the Eucharistic Prayer). Breathing with both lungs of Bible and prayer delivers the most spiritual oxygen and support to the rest of the bodily functions, making our corporal works of mercy, care for the poor, the sick, and the imprisoned effective and delivered with spiritual muscle and vitality. For Anglicans throughout history, the principal way we have breathed with both lungs of prayer and Scripture has been through inhabiting the daily offices. Inhabiting such patterns of prayer precedes the development of passions that fuel the rehabilitation of communities.

Prayer and study of Scripture stand theologically prior to other critical and missional expressions of the Body of Christ in the same way a fountainhead directs the movement and flow of water in a beautiful fountain. "Faith is the fountain of prayers," St. Augustine said. Why then do our fountains run dry? Is it because we forsake the very practices of faith that ensure that channels of living water still flow?

The spiritual synergy formed at the intersection of prayer and Scripture was certainly a principal concern of the reformers' vision, especially Thomas Cranmer, whose leadership and faithfulness is embedded in the prayer book tradition. This vision is evident in the Preface to the 1549 Book of Common Prayer:

> There was never any thing by the wit of man so well devised, or so sure established, which (in continuance of time) hath not been corrupted: as (among other things) it may plainly appear by the common prayers in the Church, commonly called Divine Service. The first original and ground whereof, if a man would search out by the ancient Fathers, he shall find that the same was not ordained but of a good purpose, and for a great advancement of godliness: For they so ordered the matter, that all the whole Bible (or the greatest part thereof) should be read over in the year; intending thereby, that the Clergy, and especially such as were Ministers of the

congregation, should (by often reading, and med-
itation of God's word) be stirred up to godliness
themselves and be more able to exhort others by
wholesome doctrine, and to confute them that were
adversaries to the truth. And further, that the people (by daily hearing of Holy Scripture read in the
Church) should continually profit more and more
in the knowledge of God, and be the more inflamed
with the love of his true religion.

It is, in part, this vision that fuels my desire to launch the offices
in my parish. Now, to be fair, we have always been a *praying* parish, a
community of people who care about prayer, and certainly long before I arrived. We have been a place fueled by programs on spiritual
disciplines, which have given rise to evangelical fervor for Scripture,
and a passion to invite others into being, as Søren Kierkegaard said,
not merely admirers but followers of Jesus. However, in the last 14
months we have gone all in on our conviction that prayer is the fountainhead of our common life. We held a conference on prayer. I have
written regular devotions on prayer. We did a small-group program
on praying the Psalms, and a class on the Book of Common Prayer,
and an Advent series on praying the offices. We held a women's Epiphany dinner and a separate men's gathering, both based on prayer. All
of this brings us to the point of the divine offices and their shape in
the Anglican tradition.

I suppose it is anachronistic to envision some golden age
when *all* of England prayed the offices together. One will search in
vain for such a moment, and we should be careful to avoid misread-

ing the past. Anglican communities of prayer have always waxed and waned, depending on the fervor and faithfulness of clergy, lay leaders, and (throughout much of history) those in religious orders. How far we have come, however, from the days when all clergy were required to pray the offices by virtue of their vows, and to do so publicly so that laypersons had the opportunity to do the same. For approximately three quarters of the history of the church, praying the divine offices was an "essential function" of the job description for Christian leadership in the church in its Latin, Eastern, and English/Anglican iterations.

Indeed, one could make the argument, as some have, that the offices stretch back to Jesus and even further to the patterns of Israel, whose rhythms of prayer were rooted in divinely mandated festivals, and set times of praying at morning, noon, and night (cf. Ps. 1:2; Dan. 6:10; Acts 3:1). We know that prayer was ordered, and done *in common*, as the disciples and apostles are cited as frequently praying "in one accord" (Acts 1:14; 2:42, 46; 4:24). Finally, we know Jesus was given to praying at both day and night (Mark 1:35; 6:46 Matt. 14:23). This cumulative weight of piety and history stands behind Cranmer's vision for daily prayer, which is summed up by Bishop Anthony Burton:

> Cranmer drew upon elements of the eight daily offices (chiefly the versions used at Salisbury Cathedral) but the project was more than a simplifying of what was already there. He believed strongly that holiness involved entering into the Gospel. So he set about to create offices at which people could

> drink deeply and systematically from the Bible. At
> the same time he also fashioned these offices so that
> people would worship God according to princi-
> ples of worship he found in the Bible itself. While
> Cranmer possessed a vast patristic scholarship, he
> was more concerned with the substance of apostolic
> worship than its forms.

We are thirsty at St. Francis in the Fields for this cool, living, nourishing, unconquerable, and sometimes tumultuous water of the Word that I hope our people will taste in the offices. Thus, we find ourselves living out a soft launch of the daily offices in our parish. We have recruited ten lay leaders and additional lectors, along with our clergy team, and we are treating this almost like a church plant within our parish. Martin Thornton would have called this "the remnant." Either way, our launch team is learning how to officiate, and we are working out the kinks of holding daily morning and evening prayer before we launch to the wider parish in the season of Lent.

Those involved love it, even if a few of them find it intimidating at first. Our officiants span a range of ages. More than half are younger than 45, and all identify as zealous converts to the prayer book tradi-tion. In addition to our clergy team, we have a helicopter mechanic, a hospice chaplain, a salesperson, a tech consultant, an accountant, two doctors, a social worker, and several retired laypersons who are passionate about this vision, each being trained to officiate, and each possessing varying degrees of experience with the prayer book. Some have prayed the offices for decades, and some only for a few weeks. In a very real sense, the offices are becoming the training ground and laboratory for lay leadership development, creating space for some to test a call to ordained leadership, while affording others the opportunity to express the priestly call given to them simply by being made in the *imago Dei*, a call that has been vivified through their plunge into the baptismal waters.

At times the offices are accompanied with dinosaurs, or the scribbling of crayons on a page, simply another expression of *ora et labora*, as children come in tow with those who are training to train others to form a *house of prayer* (Luke 19). My hope is that amid roars of the T. rex and strokes of Crayola, they too come to know the mystery Hans Urs von Balthasar articulated:

> We must be vividly aware of this mystery as we pray, contemplating the word of God: that the whole compact solidity of our creaturely being and essence, and of the everyday world in which we find ourselves and find our bearings, is afloat like a ship above the immense depths of an entirely different element ... namely the unfathomable love of the Father. The person who prays must experience the freedom of this love; not only the freedom which corresponds to the non-necessity, the contingence of his own existence, but the much deeper and wholly new and different freedom which accords with the Father's "good pleasure": we, his creatures and servants, are to be regarded and "esteemed" as members of his household, as his children and "co-heirs" with his Son. From the very outset, the coher-

ence, correctness and justice of this logic, this way of thinking and evaluating, presupposes and embraces the whole medium of ineffable grace, a presupposition shared by even the most formal grammatical component of God's language. Anyone who has ever sensed this fundamental mystery underlying our existence will take the necessity of prayer for granted ... (*Prayer*, p. 43-44)

May they take the necessity of prayer for granted as well. For we have stressed all along as a parish that prayer and praying together is not one program among many, but is instead the very wellspring of our common life together, the very waters upon which we are guided to God's New Covenant shores. It is in praying where the habituated reception of the Spirit's indwelling power and presence is unfurled into our lives. Like a sail catching wind for the first time, and every time, the offices allow us to hoist the sails, not to speed along in our own strength, but to be precisely those who are empowered by the apostolic wind behind (and ahead of) the ark of our parish, who are sent along the waves of God's providential workings in human history, always aware that "the Lord sits enthroned over the flood" (Ps. 29).

Breathing with both lungs of Scripture and prayer in the offices allows us to not only be *inspired* (inspirited) by God, but to die to ourselves *daily*, to be *expired*, so the Spirit, the breath of God, might flow out of us over the waters around us, bringing order out of the chaos of our communities. So many of our people ride the week like a white water rapid while awaiting the lazy river that is the weekend. Nevertheless, we are testing a different approach in recognizing that each morning and evening are like the eddy of a river, where — if only for a moment — we rest in the swirling currents of grace, in order to be thrust back out again into the stream of carpool lines and surgeries, grocery shopping and conflict resolution, board meetings and Netflix. For these activities *also* empty into the sea of God's purposes, who is working in all things for the good of those who love him. Conceived as such, the offices are then not a departure from how we normally live, but are a glimpse into how we should always live, attuned to the God who is closer to us than we are to ourselves.

In other words, we who are *incurvatus se* — the grain of whose hearts runs against the hard wood of the cross — are being tutored in *being* fully human before God. The cross is our rudder through these waters, Christ himself being bound to the mast, fully God, fully human. The world has long forgotten how to *be*, yet alone how to be *human*. We are seeking to sit still, and to remember the echo of Eden. We hear it chiefly in Scripture, the lessons, and especially the Psalms. Our hearts burn within us as we see full humanity shot through with full divinity on every page of sacred writ.

As we recite the Psalms, they form within us the habits of placing ourselves *fully* before the God who is already present to us. Indeed, the Psalms invite us to place even those unsavory bits of our being before the God who knows about them anyway. The Psalms remind us that we were once naked without shame before God, even as we stand stripped bare before God again, as we hear in the Collect for Purity within our eucharistic liturgy: "Almighty God, unto whom all hearts are open, all desires known, and from whom no secrets are hid" (BCP, p. 323).

We are formed, therefore; disciplined, one might say, by the lectionary. We learn to hear passages sing together as a chorus of the saving works of God. Moreover, we learn how to feel, how to love, hate, lament, cry, remember, long, delight, listen, repent, exclaim, forgive, fume, and rejoice; in short, how to be alive to what resides under the dark waters of our souls and subconscious selves. Of the Psalms, the 17th-century Anglican dean Thomas Comber wrote:

> They are called the instrument of virtue, the marrow of divinity, the storehouse of devotion, the epitome of Holy Scripture. They contain excellent forms to bless the people, to praise God, to rejoice in his favor, to bewail his absence, to confess our Faith, to crave pardon of our sins, deliverance from our enemies, and all blessings for the Church of God. In the use of them we ought to exercise all graces, repentance and faith, love and fear of God, charity to all men, and compassion to the miserable. The composition of them declares they are fitted for men of all ages and degrees, in all estates and conditions, young and old; kings, priests, and people; in prosperity and adversity; here they may find that which so exactly suits them all, as if their condition had been foreseen and particularly provided for. (*Prayerbook Spirituality*, p. 153)

We are learning how to be honest about our darkness, and honest about the tragedies of our lives. I once heard Oliver O'Donovan address the moral challenge resident in Psalm 137, a psalm of mass slaughter and forgiveness. O'Donovan said, "If one has never burned with terrible loss, one can never know what it feels like to be relieved of it." The divine offices take us there, among other destinations of the soul that stands at full spread before God.

For when we pray, we are standing at the threshold where heaven meets earth; the place where God's kingdom is coming *on earth as it is in heaven*, the nexus where this inbreaking reality takes hold of our hearts (as we feel), our minds (as we know), our bodies (as we kneel), and our souls (as we give ourselves fully to God). We may feel that nothing is happening, or we may, like the Narnian children, step into the magical wardrobe and discover the life that is more real and holistically nourishing than the fumes that fuel our mechanized, excarnate and increasingly disembodied existence.

So as the church spins about creating social collaboratives, and food truck ministries, which may have their proper place, I am convicted and convinced we can grow a healthy, humble, and faithful church that changes its community most effectively by refusing to reinvent the wheel. The gifts for our renewal lie within our own tradition — *ad fontes*! If we have the courage to forgo the "shiny new thing," we may just find our Lord himself, waiting in the boat, ready to take us to sea, ready to take us fishing once again; ready to take us to his fireside meal, where, having worked in the waters all our long days, we may know also the blazing warmth of his Communion, even amid the coldness and the darkness of the night.

Fr. Clint Wilson is the Rector of St. Francis in the Fields in Louisville, KY.

TWENTY-ONE

Bring Back the Greeks

Leander Harding

I have a talk on modernity and mission in which I try to diagnose the challenge of modernity and lay out a strategy for an effective encounter between our Western, modern context and the gospel. Here is a brief descriptive list of the steps in this missionary strategy:

1. Bring back the Greeks. Learn philosophy. Learn to ask and answer with the sophistication of Plato and Aristotle the great questions about the nature of being, truth, goodness, and beauty and about the nature of a truly good and human life. The gospel provides answers to questions that are not being asked.

Recently I had a philosophical encounter. I was picked up by a Lyft driver at the local airport. I had on my clericals and the driver asked me what I did for a living. I said I was a priest. What is that? But what do you do? Then, do you mind if I choose the music? I said, your choice. He chose very rank and vulgar rap. I am a child of the '60s and thought I couldn't be shocked, but I was wrong. When we got to my destination, I said, do you think the men singing those songs are happy? There was absolute silence and stillness. I could see my driver was really thinking. Finally, he said, I know that one guy is happy because I saw the video and he had 20 women around him. Oh, I said, is that happiness? Will it be happiness in five years, in 10, in 20? More silence. More stillness. My friend was thinking. He was thinking about a question to which the Christian faith has profound answers. It was an effective missionary encounter. He had been left with a question that has the power to draw him toward Christ. Bring back the Greeks. Study philosophy. The synergy between Greek rationalism and the gospel is not a disposable accident of history but the providence of God. See Pope Benedict XVI's Regensburg speech.

2. Pursue a radical Christocentrism. Resist the temptation to make Jesus Christ an ancillary to some other and greater good. The prosperity gospel is one example of this. Jesus the bearer of a purely political agenda, whether of the left or the right, is another. Jesus Christ is not the means to some other end. He is the Alpha and the Omega.

3. Cultivate holiness. Our proclamation must have not only the form of godliness but the power thereof.

4. Save beautiful churches. People are still drawn to cathedrals and beautiful churches, and a performance of *Messiah* will still fill a church in the midst of the secular city. The path to God through beauty is a path that has a particular appeal for moderns who are being choked by the ugly and the banal.

5. As part of paving the path to God through beauty, there is a need to inhabit and transmit Christian culture. The church needs to reach out to the cultures she is trying to evangelize, but the church is a cult with a culture and has its own art and architecture and music and literature. In the past, the task of the transmission of this culture could be shared with schools, universities, museums, and concert halls. The transmission of the high culture of the church needs to be an increasingly important part of our Christian formation.

6. Pray the Great Thanksgiving. Modernity is characterized by the posture of grievance. There is about modernity more than a hint of the world-weariness and cosmic disgust of ancient Gnosticism. Modern utopians regard the world as we find it odious and beyond redemption. It must be all wiped away so that the new will arise. The world is to be escaped rather than blessed in thanksgiving. Counting blessings is a fundamental Christian spiritual discipline, and one with a healing power for modern angst. A joyful and grateful people are the proper carriers of the good news of the gospel.

7. Be disarmed and disarming. The peaceable kingdom is not

brought about by the violence of men but by the nonviolence of God. The means of evangelism and mission must be consistent with the sacrificial love of the cross. Love returned for love is the aim as we invite others to know the love wherewith we are loved. Scorn and dismissive rhetoric are counter-evangelical. Moralistic hectoring of all forms is a kind of violence.

8. Foster a Christocentric ecumenical witness. On the missionary frontier, denominational divides are counter-evangelical. Lesslie Newbigin has rightly pointed out that we cannot tell men and women that there is one family of God and do so credibly from a divided platform. The only principle that can mend ecumenical division is an ecumenical Christocentrism. Ecumenical proclamation of mere Christianity will have missionary power in an increasingly tribal modernity. The ecumenical challenge is now as much within churches as it is between churches.

9. Cultivate Marian spirituality. The signature song of modernity is "I Did It My Way." Mary is characterized by attention to Scripture, suppleness in the hands of the Holy Spirit and an openness and surrender to God's way. Mary is the antidote to the modern sickness of the autonomous self-run riot. Her disappearance from the iconography and spirituality of many churches is a symptom of accommodation to modernity and the recovery of her presence as the spirit of a church that says, "Behold the handmaid of the Lord," is essential for a church that can feed and nurture its children and be faithful in the face of a world that rejects her Lord.

10. Aim for transcendent liturgy. Transcendence is in God's hand, but we can prepare for it and aim for it. Dostoevsky says that low ceilings are bad for the soul. Modern people seldom look up. Liturgy that by God's grace opens the doors of heaven has a converting power. When any kind of evangelism and Christian education was prohibited in the Soviet Union, people were still converted by coming in from the gray Soviet street to a liturgy full of light, beauty, mystery, and life.

I close with a passage from the late ecumenical theologian Robert Jenson in his essay "How the World Lost Its Story."

> One of many analogies between postmodernity and dying antiquity—in which the church lived for her most creative period—is that the late antique world also insisted on being a meaningless chaos, and that the church had to save her converts by offering herself as the narratable world within which life could be lived with dramatic coherence. … The church so constituted herself in her *liturgy*. … The classic liturgical action of the church was not about anything else at all; it was itself the reality about which truth could be told. … In the postmodern world, if a congregation or churchly agency wants to be "relevant," here is the first step: It must recover the classic liturgy of the church, in all its dramatic density, sensual actuality, and brutal realism, and make this the one exclusive center of its life. In the postmodern world,

all else must at best be decoration and more likely distraction.

The Very Rev. Dr. Leander S. Harding, dean of the Cathedral of All Saints in Albany, is entering his fourth decade as a priest of the Episcopal Church.

TWENTY-TWO

Tightly Woven: Anglican Parishes and Religious Orders

Mark Michael

A battered old crucifix hangs on the wall beside my desk. It's no great artistic treasure: chipped wood, an iron, machine-made corpus, a bit of chain. It's just like the thousands of other crosses that graced the walls of pious Victorians. Except this is a cross from a nun's cell, the focus of prayer for women who gave their lives out of love for Christ and in service to his Church, generation after generation, praying for priests like me.

It was given to me by the man who preached the sermon at my ordination to the priesthood. Father Philip was a mentor to me during my time at seminary in England, and in addition to serving as principal of Pusey House, he was the last warden of Ascot Priory in Berkshire, the convent of one of Anglicanism's first religious orders.

I went with him to keep the Triduum at Ascot during my seminary days, where I enjoyed a few talks with Mother Cecilia of the Resurrection, the last of her order. She had entered religious life in 1935, when my grandmother was a toddler. But at the time Father Philip gave me the cross, Mother Cecilia had recently died, and the convent was being reordered. The cross was from one of the old cells.

"For years," Father Philip said, "the sisters prayed that God would send the Church faithful priests. They were praying for you." That cross challenges and encourages me. It reminds of the great trust I bear and of my responsibility to be faithful in my call. But it also helps me recognize that in my work I am upheld and sustained by the prayers of so many brothers and sisters, many of them far holier than I will ever be. It also points to a deep connection between parish ministry and the religious life, which has been one of Anglicanism's greatest treasures in the last several generations.

When religious life was reestablished in the Anglican Communion in the 1840s, it was primarily a parish-based ministry. The Society of the Holy Trinity, which eventually made its home at Ascot, had begun as the Devonport Sisters of Mercy, based in a parish at the Plymouth Docks. In the great spirit of Victorian activism, the community founded "a home for delinquent boys, two refuges for training girls for domestic service, an industrial school, six lodging houses for poor families, five ragged schools, a soup kitchen and a home for old sailors." When Florence Nightingale sailed for the front in Crimea to found modern nursing, nearly half her crew were Devonport Sisters.

Religious communities like these, which carried out extensive work among the poor and distressed, were deeply rooted in the day-to-day life of Anglican parish churches. They taught Sunday school and catechism classes, arranged flowers and ironed altar linens, attended daily prayers and visited the housebound. Many became trusted friends and confidants, ordinary examples of Christ's call to generous sacrifice and humble service. And, of course, they prayed.

Anti-Catholic bigotry was a deeply rooted feature of middle 19th-century England, and the first generation of Anglican nuns was roundly criticized in some quarters. But the hostility did not prove long lasting. The nuns' heroic labors won the affection of the public in an age of social activism. Surely, their association with ordinary churchgoers and the rather haphazardly local way in which they were founded were not inconsequential. Anglican religious orders have never been particularly rich or powerful, and until the last generation or two, they have rarely been secluded. The deep rivalries between monastic and parish life that have sometimes marked Roman Catholic and Orthodox history have never really developed among us.

An order of Episcopal nuns operated a diocesan orphanage for many decades in the community in upstate New York where I last served as rector. Though it was technically independent, the ties between it and the parish were close. Older parishioners would speak of nuns marching their charges down the street to attend the Sunday Mass. Old parish registers record weekly services in the orphanage chapel, and for many years the orphans accounted for half the baptisms. One young woman from the parish tried a vocation with the community, and though she returned back "into the world" after a year or so (a block down the street, that was), she remained a deeply committed Christian the rest of her life, living simply and helping with church work of every imaginable kind.

The orphanage didn't survive the financial crisis of the 1930s, and the nuns returned to their motherhouse in Canada. But many, many decades later, a few of my oldest parishioners still spoke fondly of the sisters who had taught Sunday school and trained them for "altar work." Seventy years after the nuns had departed, their witness continued to inspire.

In times of dramatically diminished vocations and aging communities, only a handful of Episcopal monks and nuns remained in our parishes. But some orders continue in ministries of spiritual direction and generous hospitality to the clergy and laity. They open their homes to guests and their chapels to fellow worshipers. Many continue in their foundational vocation to ministry among the poor, while others, like the Society of Saint John the Evangelist, have devoted considerable resources to teaching the faith in innovative ways. My own ministry has been richly blessed by the friendship, counsel, and prayers of monks and nuns.

But we do not rely on them as much as we once did; something profound has been lost. I remember vividly a conversation with a former spiritual director, a nun of All Saints Convent in Catonsville, Maryland, when most of her community was received into the Roman Catholic Church in 2009. It didn't come as a surprise to anyone; the All Saints Sisters had determinedly resisted most of the Episcopal Church's recent innovations. "They no longer seem to want what we can offer," the sister said to me.

Decades before, they had hosted diocesan clergy days and discernment retreats. There was a reliable stream of local Episcopalians in the pews for Sunday vespers. But for some time they had been (mostly) politely ignored. The sisters hoped that in another communion, one with a longer tradition and deeper understanding of monastic life, there would be a warmer welcome for them, an openness to their wisdom about the way of Christ.

I hope that they have found it, but I also think we need them and others like them within the Episcopal Church. Like so many others, I am very hopeful about the emphasis on evangelization and parish renewal that is at the center of our new Presiding Bishop's agenda. Spurred by the challenging call of Episcopal Resurrection's Memorial to the Church and the TREC Report, we seem more eager than ever to help congregations focus on our core work of following Jesus together into the community, traveling lightly. Our brothers and sisters in the religious life, whose discipleship is framed by the "evangelical counsels," surely are among those best equipped to lead us.

General Convention's decision last summer to prioritize church planting and congregational redevelopment is an important step in the right direction. Perhaps we also need an expanded focus on developing parish-based monastic (and new monastic) communities, and on providing greater support for those doing innovative work. Some exciting new initiatives have cropped up in recent years, including Community of the Franciscan Way in Durham, North Carolina, and the Community of St. Anselm, the Archbishop of Canterbury's institute at Lambeth Palace for young people. Perhaps churchwide vocations conferences (a follow-up to Bishop Curry's revival meetings?) would be a way forward, or initiatives that gather the wisdom of the historic communities for new settings. Could each diocese aim to plant and support one new parish-based religious community in the next five years?

New programs are helpful in the work of renewal, but transformed people are essential. God has raised up great saints and wise leaders from people in all walks of life. But there is something particularly valuable about the intensity and steadfastness of those who live the religious life, which can draw people to Christ and pull together a community in service to him. If the "Jesus Movement" has squad leaders, monks and nuns must be in their number.

When I look at my cross, I thank God for those nuns whose prayers sustain the work I do. I pray also for those like them who remain in their vitally important vocation today. I pray also that someday, one of my own flock will follow them, or better yet, that there will be a whole community of nuns or monks working alongside me as I tend the flock and take the Gospel into the world.

The Rev. Mark Michael is editor-in-chief of The Living Church. *An Episcopal priest, he has reported widely on global Anglicanism, and also writes about church history, liturgy, and pastoral ministry.*

TWENTY-THREE

Evangelism: Tackling the Roots of Episcopalians' Reluctance

Titus Presler

Will you proclaim by word and example the good news of God in Christ?" Episcopalians are asked this question at every baptism celebrated according to the liturgies of the 1979 Book of Common Prayer. "Word and example" — the phrase refers obviously to speech and action, and it echoes the common pairing of "word and deed."

Episcopalians rhetorically affirm a connection between word and example, speech and deed. When it comes to practice, though, we typically say *yes* to example, *yes* to deed, but *no* to word, or, at best, *maybe* to word. Reticence about verbalizing the good news of God in Christ in actual speech is what underlies Episcopalians' reluctance to engage in evangelism, still less to embrace it as a mandate for ourselves or for the Church as a whole.

Evangelism labors under weighty negative impressions of it: intrusive fundamentalists knocking on your door and telling you that only their version of the gospel and their church are acceptable to God. Televangelists who seem more concerned with raising money for themselves than with the welfare of their flock. Telling rather than listening. Arrogance and imposition rather than humility and affirmation.

It's startling, then, that Presiding Bishop Michael Curry has made evangelism a centerpiece of his ministry within the church and beyond. He quips that, for him, the title of CEO means that he's the church's Chief Evangelism Officer. The church now has a robust Evangelism Initiative, headed by Canon Stephanie Spellers and Jerusalem Greer. Periodic Evangelism Matters conferences are catalyzing evangelism initiatives in dioceses and congregations. Regional revival meetings highlight Bishop Curry's stirring oratory, striking theology and delightful humor.

The initiative's irenic and appealing definition of evangelism has the potential to disarm the concerns of the wary: "Evangelism is the spiritual practice of seeking, naming, and celebrating Jesus' loving presence in the stories of all people, and then inviting them to more." Here evangelism is seen as a spiritual practice, a prayerful orientation to God and the world, rather than as an aggressive program. The evangelist listens, confident that God, even Jesus, is already there in the experience of the other. The evangelist affirms and celebrates and avoids minimizing or dismissing the spirituality of the other. The evangelist discovers treasure in the experience of the other and finds her own faith challenged and enlarged. And then, yes, the evangelist invites the other to more, whatever that may be: to form or deepen a relationship with God in Christ, to express faith through a social justice initiative, to grow spiritually in a church community — whatever might be appropriate.

Episcopalians are intrigued as well as surprised by these developments. Certainly Bishop Curry's sermon at the royal wedding in 2018 gave the church a heads-up that joyful gospel proclamation is compatible with being Episcopalian. Many church members are similarly inspired by the spontaneous faith-sharing among Anglican companions they encounter on short-term mission trips in Africa, Asia, Latin America and Oceania.

Nevertheless many Episcopalians hesitate to engage in conversations about spirituality and faith in their own contexts, and they resist appeals to become more evangelistic, whether in their personal practice or the life of their congregations. Many factors are in play, and they highlight ways in which gospel reticence is inconsistent with faithful Christian practice.

What are those inconsistencies? Christian reluctance about verbal proclamation is, in short, linguistically nonsensical, historically amnesiac, genealogically disrespectful, and liturgically inconsistent. It is cognitively incoherent, culturally conformist, ecclesially establishmentarian, inter-religiously isolationist and missionally incomplete. Here I elaborate each of these critiques. Reluctance about the verbal proclamation we promise in the Baptismal Covenant is *linguistically nonsensical* because it ignores the self-evident reference to speech in the verb "proclaim," which is derived from the Latin *proclamare,* meaning to "cry out." It is the "good news" of God in Christ that we undertake to proclaim as the baptized. News by definition is something people tell, broadcast or print.

The good news of God in Christ is not simply a principle or an attitude but a *story,* a narrative, a news story that begins in creation, continues through the struggles of Israel, culminates in the incarnation of God in Jesus, the word made flesh, and continues in the Spirit-filled life of the Church. Yes, one's faithfulness to the import of this story will be verified (or not) by how one lives, but the story itself is news that requires telling, verbal communication, in order for it to be known. To imagine that deed alone can tell a story is illusory. Note also that the baptismal promise is about "word and example" rather than "word and deed." An example of what? — well, of faithful living that shows forth the import of the story. That is, our actions as the baptized are linked to our words by exemplifying, illustrating, what we are assumed to have proclaimed verbally.

Reluctance about verbal proclamation is *historically amnesiac.* Word and deed were both prominent in the ministry of Jesus. Matthew's introduction to Jesus' impact in Galilee includes both in equal measure: "Jesus went throughout Galilee, teaching in their synagogues and proclaiming the good news of the kingdom and curing every disease and every sickness among the people" (4:23). As a result, the ordinary Christian today can pretty instantly recollect both various things that Jesus said and various things that Jesus did. Word and deed alike were prominent in the early ministry of the disciples as recorded by Luke in Acts. Word and deed have both been prominent in the mission of virtually all churches throughout the history of the Christian movement as evangelistic proclamation was accompanied by work in education, healthcare, social liberation, and economic development. Given this consistent history, on what basis can we arrogate to ourselves the privilege of dismissing verbal witness in favor of example alone? When we do so we are distorting our Christian DNA and distorting the image of the God within us who is the God of word as well as deed.

Episcopalians often have recourse to the aphorism attributed to Francis of Assisi: "Preach at all times. Use words when necessary." The saying does not square with Jesus' example, or Francis' own practice, for that matter. A stress on example *instead* of word is often appropriate in settings where verbal witness incurs risk to life and limb, as in many parts of the Muslim world today. I recently heard the aphorism repeated by a friend in Pakistan, where evangelism is indeed risky. For the average Episcopalian, however, the Francis quote is simply a license for complacent silence.

Reluctance about verbal proclamation is *genealogically disrespectful*. Every Christian is a Christian by virtue of *someone's* verbal witness as well as witness by example. Some have become Christian through hearing the gospel in their own life story as children, teenagers, or adults. Even those who cannot remember *not* being Christian have still learned the gospel story verbally at some point. And their family heritage began at some time in the past when someone became a Christian for the first time through someone else's witness and then passed the faith on to their descendants. Dismissing verbal witness today as unimportant disrespects the experience of our forebears who became Christian through hearing and embracing the gospel story.

Reluctance about verbal proclamation is *liturgically inconsistent,* especially for Episcopalians. Upon arriving at church on Sunday, Episcopalians encounter a virtual deluge of biblical and liturgical word. We hear not just one scripture, but three plus a psalm. The canticles are steeped in Scripture. The typical four hymns are poetic and musical masterpieces. The sermon is of course a verbal event, and the prayers of the liturgy are eloquent and compelling. The average Episcopalian enjoys all this and is proud of it. Many have become Episcopalians partly because of the liturgy's attention to precision and eloquence. Yet our worship is designed not only to inspire us in the sanctuary but also to strengthen our witness in the world, an intention that we affirm over and over again in our prayers. The third Collect for Mission at Morning Prayer is just one instance of many: "So clothe us in your Spirt that we, reaching out our hands in love, may bring those who do not know you to the knowledge and love of you." It is strikingly inconsistent, therefore, to so glory in the riches of word in church and then dismiss the importance continuing that verbal stream of faith outside the walls of the church as we enter into conversation with people in our communities and workplaces. True, the liturgy itself has catalyzed the faith journey of many, but our evangelism should not end at the organ's last note.

Reluctance about verbal proclamation is *cognitively incoherent.* Our cognition is bound up with language, and this to such an extent that child psychologists are still working to unpack the nature of pre-verbal children's thinking, precisely because they cannot speak. Certain levels of thought require words. So, why are many Episcopalians in a quandary when it comes to putting what they believe into words? Is it that they don't know what they believe, and therefore are unable to verbalize it? Mark Preece, a rector in Vermont, turns that assumption on its head: "No, they don't know what they believe because they don't talk about it!" It is often through speaking that we come to know what we believe. This is why some of the most helpful exercises in the current evangelism initiative are those where participants pair up to tell each other, in two or three minutes, how they came to faith, or what their understanding of the gospel is.

Reluctance about verbal proclamation is *culturally conformist*. Many Episcopalians pride themselves on being counter-cultural in their politics, social views, and artistic tastes. Avoiding faith discussion, however, is a vivid instance of cultural conformity, especially in the relatively well-educated circles in which many Episcopalians move. Of the three topics that the old cliché would have us avoid in polite company, religion may be more taboo today than either politics or sex. Moreover, the civic code of separating church from state in the United States has, for many, driven religion out of the public square altogether and confined it to a purely private sphere of personal opinion and devotion. When spirituality and religion are culturally sequestered as private matters, bringing them out into the relatively public setting of even a casual conversation with an acquaintance can feel like breaking a taboo, violating a code. Not so among Jesus's disciples: "We cannot keep from speaking about what we have seen and heard," declared Peter and John to the elders of Jerusalem (Acts 4:20).

Reluctance about verbal proclamation is *ecclesially establishmentarian*. When George Whitefield and John Wesley, both Anglican clergy, started the evangelistic revival movement in the 18th century that came to be known as Methodism, the institutional church held them in such contempt that the movement ultimately felt compelled to form a new denomination. Going out to preach in streets and fields was thought to be undignified and populist in the Church of England, which was "established" in the sense of being the official church of the state. Though not established in these United States, the Episcopal Church has inherited an establishmentarian ethos: "Our doors are open. Our liturgy is so eloquent and our music so beautiful! How can you help but become one of us?" Many a vestry discussion of evangelism has devolved to redesigning the building's outdoor signage and reorganizing the leaflet to make the liturgy more accessible. The focus shifts to attracting visitors and welcoming them in to become part of our group. That is the establishmentarian orientation of a now long outmoded Christendom.

As Dutch missiologist Johannes Blauw pointed out, that is centripetal mission, as in the world coming to Zion in the Old Testament, whereas New Testament mission, beginning with Jesus himself, is centrifugal: moving outward, crossing boundaries, encountering difference. Evangelism goes out beyond the church community to engage people in the dimension of spirituality. Doing so feels exposed and risky, because then we are a minority, maybe a sole voice, amid a possibly indifferent and secular majority. It is prophetic, the opposite of establishmentarian. The purpose is not to convert others, by the way, for that is the work of the Holy Spirit, and still less to make them church members, though that is a blessing if it happens. The purpose is rather, in the current Episcopal formulation, to "seek, name, and celebrate Jesus' loving presence in the stories of all people, and then invite them to more."

Reluctance about verbal proclamation is *inter-religiously isolationist*. The prominence of inter-religious distrust, conflict and violence is a major challenge of the 21st century in virtually all regions of the world, including North America. Many Christians of good will are reluctant to discuss faith with strangers lest they find that their conversation partner is a Muslim, Jew, Hindu, Buddhist, Sikh, or Bahai who may be offended by Christian expression. The reality is quite different. Not so affected by the US American secular paradigm that privatizes religion, people of other religions are often delighted to converse about faith, sharing their own and learning about another's. Christians who engage formally in inter-religious dialogue agree that what is helpful is not apologetic vagueness about one's own faith but forthright clarity. The solution to inter-religious conflict is not an isolationist retreat into silence but eager and humble engagement in conversation. Both physically and electronically, today's world features a vast and cacophonous dialogue about ideas and values, and religious perspectives are prominent among them. Ordinary Christian voices are needed in that dialogue, whether with the neighbor next door, the colleague at work, or the seatmate while traveling. Seeds of hope in this distraught century are sown when such conversation nurtures interfaith understanding and friendship.

Finally, reluctance about verbal proclamation is *missionally incomplete.* The sense of mission among many Episcopalians today has narrowed only to deed, and typically it focuses exclusively on projects designed to alleviate the conditions of economically poor communities. Food and water security, housing, healthcare, education, and income generation are major emphases, whether at home or abroad. Poverty alleviation and economic justice are indeed crucial mission imperatives amid the 21st century's widening gap between the rich and the poor both at home and abroad. Likewise the church's mission must urgently address the crisis of climate change and environmental degradation. The church is faithful, though, only as it is faithful to the *whole* mission that Jesus set before us: "'Go, therefore, and make disciples of all nations. . . .' . . . He sent them out to proclaim the kingdom of God and to heal. . . . 'You will be my witnesses . . .'" (Matt.

28:19; Luke 9:2; Acts 1:11). Episcopalians often screen out one side of the New Testament's combination of proclamation and example, one side of the Christian movement's twin emphases of evangelism and loving service to those in need. As a result, the Episcopal Church has a reputation for beautiful liturgy within our walls and social service beyond our walls, but few come to know Jesus through our sharing the gospel story with them. And we ourselves miss out on the spiritual growth we might experience through engaging with the spiritualities we would discover in conversation with others.

At a seminary I led there is a student residence where the open design puts all apartment doors on the outside and hence accessible to the public. One Saturday morning I received a phone call from a seminarian who was offended that two members of a local church had knocked on her door to invite a conversation about spirituality and faith. Could I as the dean do something to stop this happening? I was reminded of Moses' response to Joshua's request, "Stop them!" when two miscellaneous Israelites began prophesying in the wilderness camp: "Would that all the Lord's people were prophets, and that the Lord would put his Spirit upon them!" (Num. 11:29). Would that all God's people were evangelists! For that is our call — and our promise.

Titus Presler, vicar of St. Matthew's Church in Enosburg Falls, Vermont, is convener of Green Mountain Witness, the evangelism initiative of the Diocese of Vermont, and president of the Global Episcopal Mission Network. Former president of the Seminary of the Southwest, he blogs at TitusOnMission.wordpress.com.

TWENTY-FOUR

Raising Your Church's Profile in Your Town

Neal Michell

In my role as canon to the ordinary, it was my responsibility to visit all the churches in our diocese on a consistent basis. My standard practice for churches in rural areas and small towns was to drive to the town, visit a local coffee shop, order coffee, and ask the waitperson or cashier if they could give me directions to the local Episcopal Church. Seldom did anyone even know the name of the parish, much less how to get there.

I have been involved in the discernment of people exploring ordination to the priesthood for the past 20 years. It is becoming increasingly difficult to find people who either want — or are even willing — to consider serving a church in a small town away from the larger cities and suburbs. That is a shame. Serving as priest in a small town can be greatly rewarding and, really, a lot of fun. Although I have served churches in cities and towns of just about every population size — rural areas (population 2,400 to 4,000), small town (7,000), largish town (31,000), suburb (40,000), and city (5.5 million) — I have found the smaller towns the easiest to get involved in, through community organizations, and thus the easiest places to raise our parish's profile. This essay will cover the things I have learned about raising a church's profile in towns with populations of 2,500 to 40,000.

How does a church raise its profile in the community?

1. *Network through Parishioners.* Raising the church's profile starts with the priest. Often, many parishioners are already engaged in the community in a variety of ways, but when a priest does so, it heightens the awareness of all the church's volunteer efforts in the community and can serve as a doorway for the priest to volunteer as well. In one town I served in, a parishioner was the head of the school board and invited me to speak at the teacher orientation. In another community, a parishioner was the valedictorian that year and invited me to speak at the baccalaureate service for the graduating seniors.

2. *Newspapers are invaluable.* Introduce yourself to the editor of your local newspaper. Yes, many small towns still have a local newspaper, and it is the major medium for communication and still plays an important role in community awareness and cohesion. Here are some suggestions for working with the local newspapers.

- Buy ads. People in smaller towns do read those ads, along with most everything else in the local paper. That will get the attention of editors as well, as newspaper ads are their "bread and butter."
- Offer to write an occasional commentary for the local newspaper on local or national news or societal trends. (Because your church already buys ads in the newspaper, you will be an attractive candidate for getting your opinion pieces published.)
- When asked for a comment, give it well. For example, if there is a community event, or an interdenominational community gathering, prepare your comments ahead of time. Communication is the word of the day, not erudition.

3. *Get involved in community service.* Some of these suggestions are suited for individuals, and some are appropriate for the church as an organization.

- Join the neighborhood association where you live as well as the neighborhood association where your church is located. Become known there as a servant to the community. Open your church as a place for the neighborhood association to hold its meetings.
- Volunteer to serve on community boards, such as hospice, food pantry, and so on. If the town has a service organization, such as Lions Club, or Rotary Club, and so on, by all means join one.
- Volunteer for ride-alongs with police officers. That will

provide you with wonderful stories that can raise your credibility in the community as well as raise the church's awareness of other needs.

- Serve as a mentor, a Big Brother/Big Sister, or a reading partner in your neighborhood elementary school.
- Have the church join the Chamber of Commerce and attend luncheons.
- Use illustrations in your sermons about some of your experiences serving the community and preach on the servant ministry of the church in the community. Encourage parishioners to be volunteers as servant ministers of the gospel in the community.

4. *Be involved in sports activities.* Sports involvement can be a wonderful bridge to the community. Consider these possibilities:

- Do you have extra space on your property? Often soccer teams are begging for practice fields. Consider allowing a local youth or adult soccer team to practice on your church's property.
- What is the most well-attended high school sporting event? In Texas it is football. In other areas of the country it might be basketball, baseball, or hockey. Buy season tickets and be visible at the games.

5. *Recognize that social media is as necessary as it is in a city.* The small-town priest must be a generalist, knowing about many

things. Being adept at social media is a must. Here a few of the basic "must dos" in this digital age. I'm keeping this list simple, because small churches often don't think they have resources for much social media.

- Keep your church's website up-to-date. This is not rocket science, but it is amazing how many churches still have their Holy Week service times on the front page of their website in September.
- *Facebook.* If you don't have a Facebook presence, you should. For little money you can get people directed to your website. Don't know where to turn for advice? Contact your friendly diocesan communications director. Consider asking your diocese to sponsor a webinar on social media for the small-town church.
- *Broadcasting your Sunday services.* Online services are a must, even after the pandemic. For very little money you can get your church wired and online. You say you don't have any digital experts in your church? Hire a high school sophomore for very little money who can help you broadcast your services.

6. *Try these challenges.* Some churches may want to tackle bigger challenges. Here are two:

- *Community garden.* This may not be needed in some smaller towns, but if your town has at least one apartment complex, this may be a nice fit for your church.

Building a community garden is not cheap, but it can allow your church to reach people that would not normally be reached. The community garden at our church reaches young adults, seniors, and Hispanic neighbors who are not a part of our church. We have had at least a dozen families join our church in the last 10 years through our community garden.

- *Theology on Tap.* This outreach goes by many names (because the original Theology on Tap is trademarked by the Roman Catholic Church). The idea of Theology on Tap (and its progeny) is to hold speaker series in local pubs or bars on a consistent basis.

I realize that an essay like this can be pretty intimidating. Don't be intimidated. Tackle one or two of these ideas at a time. Let your vestry wrestle with these as a group. Here are some questions for the vestry to ask itself:

- What community service organizations are members of our vestry already involved in?
- Which of these ideas are we already acting on and doing well?
- Which of these are we not doing well that we should work on?
- Which of these are we not doing well that we should quit doing?
- Which of these suggestions, if we implemented them, do we think would give us the "biggest bang for our buck"?
- Which three ideas would we like to see our church accom-

plish this year? Tally the votes of the whole vestry and develop a plan to implement these ideas.

The Very Rev. Dr. Neal Michell was born in Dallas, Texas, and grew up in Garland. Until recently, he was Prebendary in the Diocese of Dallas and Dean of St. Matthew's Cathedral in Dallas.

TWENTY-FIVE

Preaching and Imagination

Richard Kew

Not too long ago I found myself chatting with a group of lay folks about preaching. The conversations turned to the topic of imagination. These were mature, intelligent Christians who appreciate good preaching, but told me that a lot of what they hear tends to be wooden, thus failing to engage them. Their comments resonated with me. After four decades of ordained life, I moved into seminary work before finally retiring. During the last ten years I have been on the receiving end of more sermons than ever in my life, circumstances that mean I share my friends' assessment of contemporary preaching. Few preachers manage a zinger every week, but too many seem content with mediocrity. The content may be solid, but the format is bland

and colorless, failing to reach the heart and soul of the listener. What is often lacking is imagination.

Nourishing apostolic preaching is a critical part of pastoral care, and what comes from the pulpit sets the tone, vision, and direction of a congregation's life. The starting point must be seriously opening up the Scriptures, not the shallow religious rambling that too often is palmed off as "relevant" preaching. Eugene Peterson writes, "The scriptures are not a textbook on God; they are access to the living word of God that speaks a new world into being." Preaching is perhaps the primary key to help Christians hear what God is saying.

The starting point when preaching is not the audience but prayerful solitude, in the study with the Bible. It is then delivered in the context of worship, providing all present with the opportunity to listen to the Word proclaimed within a believing sacramental community. There, God's grace may drive us afresh to our knees, committing our lives once more to Christ's service before going out again into the arena of a waiting and often hostile world.

No preacher speaks from a position of personal spiritual strength, but as a redeemed sinner sharing a message from God that we have initially preached to ourselves. We have God's treasure in earthen vessels, and speak out of our own stumbling encounters with the Lord, his Word, and his mysterious ways. A preacher who is not daily nourished by God's revelation (1 Tim. 4:6) lacks the capacity to "be constant in season and out of season" (2 Tim. 4:2).

As with prayer, imagination is a vital component of the preaching task; imagination is God's gift. Speaking imaginatively to our congregation obliges us to know who they are, and demands from us the ability to understand what it is like to sit in the pew while we speak.

Preaching is less about performance than reaching for inner resources so that those listening can hear what God is saying. Imaginative preaching is about fanning the flame in our listeners' hearts so receptive imaginations willingly respond, "Lord, here am I, send me" (see Isa. 6:1-8).

Imaginative, engaging preaching within a congregation is a cumulative process. It is like the construction of a building, a holy temple to the Lord (1 Cor. 3:9-17), every week laying brick upon brick. This requires not just adequate time set aside every week for preparation, but also a longer-term preaching plan so that you know where you are going and are able to do the groundwork, the reading, thinking, and praying, not only to prepare but to keep yourself fresh.

In the pew on Sundays or in the seminary chapel, I have listened to far too many sermons that are quite awful, not only because there was little that grasped my imagination, but because it has been so blatantly obvious to this seasoned preacher that preparation has been minimal at the best. The late Bishop John Coburn of Massachusetts used to tell the story of the young priest who became fascinated by the preaching in the Acts of the Apostles. It seemed that the apostles stood up to speak and on the spot the Holy Spirit told them what to say. The priest decided to give this a try himself, so the next Sunday he took to the pulpit, opened the Bible, then asked the Spirit to speak to him. The Holy Spirit did and told him, "You're not prepared."

For the priest whose excuse is that there isn't enough time for preparation: that priest ought not to be preaching. Preparation and imagination go hand-in-hand, and require hard work. What was striking about the late Steve Jobs was the time and effort he put into preparation before launching a new product. If he went to such lengths merely to sell smartphones or computers, how much more should those of us called to preach God's Word.

Then there is the issue of application. On both sides of the Atlantic, too many messages leave the listener hanging. The message may be biblically and theologically sound but it fails to answer the question "So what?" We all need help to know how what has been said can be made to work for my own life, but the preacher gives me few clues and little guidance. Application is not telling folks what to do, but enabling them to see how they can enable the Word of God to go to work in the humdrum world of their daily lives.

Just as the best golfer regularly needs to revisit stance or grip, no preacher ever arrives, and I have discovered that what might have been appropriate in one generation has little leverage with the next. Preaching is *a lifetime spent learning and then relearning* the spiritual art of proclaiming (and living) God's message; this happens within the context of the ups and downs of our own pilgrimage. Preaching is a byproduct of our journey of faith, requiring application, study, prayer, and tons of imagination.

The Rev. Richard Kew is priest associate at St. George's Church, Nashville. He was born and raised in England, was educated at the University of London and London College of Divinity, and was ordained to the priesthood at St. Paul's Cathedral, London, in 1970.

TWENTY-SIX

Mrs. Truax and the Importance of Sunday School

Mark Michael

Thirty years ago this weekend, I was promoted. I had started first grade a week before, and, at the Rally Day assembly, I mumbled through my assigned recitation (a short poem). The Sunday School superintendent handed me a brand-new, black leather King James Bible, with my name written on the inside cover in her elegant hand. The inscription also notified me that I was now a member of the Junior Department of the Sunday School at Saint John's Church. To everyone at Saint John's, though, I was really joining "Mrs. Truax's class." It seemed even then that she had been teaching forever. She had taught my mother back in the early Sixties, when the church was brimming with Baby

Boomer children, a class in every corner of the Sunday School annex.

It was rather different on my promotion day, when amid the inevitable fluctuations of children's attendance, our congregation found itself at a low ebb. I was the only promotion we'd had in several years, and the Junior Department was to be composed of me and about a dozen sixth graders. It was rather abrupt to shift from felt boards one week to reading through the Book of Esther in seventeenth-century prose the next, but I was proud at being able (mostly) to follow the lines in my new Bible.

A few weeks later, though, things changed dramatically. The sixth graders were all confirmed, and they moved on to a class taught by someone else, over beyond the Parish Hall. That left me as Mrs. Truax's only pupil. Now by the rules that pertain in most parts of life, that should have been the end of the Junior Department. You just don't prepare a Sunday School lesson each week for one six-year-old boy. But Mrs. Truax did.

Every Sunday, throughout most of my elementary school years, she taught a class of one. And she taught me with all the skill she had developed over decades in the classroom. There was a different story each week, Bible memorization games, posters, maps, and a little piece of hard candy on the way out the door. We sang and drew pictures and once made a terrarium in a Sanka can[1]. It was a real class, with a weekly roll call, recitations on the stage three times a year, and little brass pins at Rally Day for perfect attendance. It was the highlight of my week.

She also trained me to serve as Saint John's only acolyte for the same number of years. I didn't sit in the chancel, but beside her in the

---

1   https://en.wikipedia.org/wiki/Sanka

front row. What I remember is the Lord's Prayer, the weekly canticles, and all the verses of dozens of hymns. I remember her mother who sat with us every week, the ancient and very distinguished Mrs. Weller, who wore hats covered in black netting and brandished a lacquered cane, carved with serpents. And I remember gazing at the stained glass and thinking just how important a job being an acolyte must be. I knew it brought such joy to Mrs. Truax to have me beside her, so surely (I thought) it must give glory to God as well.

Jesus once led a little child into the huddle of his disciples. "Whoever welcomes one such child in my name, welcomes me" (Mt. 18:5). *One such child* — that was me. She loved me like I was her own, like I was him whom she loved above all. She loved me with the strength he supplied, and it was through her, probably more than anyone else, that I came to find him. I learned to cherish the Bible in those years in the Junior Department, to rejoice in the worship of the Church, to turn to God in prayer. Mrs. Truax thought I would make a fine minister, and she did a great deal of the forming. When I was ordained a priest, she presented me to the bishop and was one of the first in line to receive my blessing.

I last served as rector of a parish that was part of a diocese composed mainly of small, struggling rural churches — churches like the one in which I'd grown up. Four or five times a year, at one clerical gathering or another, the bishop would urge us to have some plan for Sunday School. "You might only have one or two children," he would say, "but make sure you have something to offer them. Have somebody ready with a lesson to go in case a child shows up one Sunday." The suburban rectors would politely roll their eyes. Who could imagine a class for one child? Best to give it up when you're beaten,

I suppose. But once upon a time that one child was me, and having a teacher who cared enough to pour her best into me made all the difference in the world.

I was grateful for Bruce Robison's piece[2] a few weeks ago about the insufficiencies of Sunday School. He's absolutely right that teachers can't carry the full burden for religious formation and that many parents should take their baptismal promises far more seriously. I am deeply grateful for having parents who read me Bible stories and prayed with me every night, and who brought me with them to service every week.

But there is something unique about the way a faithful teacher can nurture faith in a person's life. After all, Saint Paul commended Timothy's mother and grandmother for teaching him the truth, but he was the young man's true spiritual father. For all Monica's prayer and tears, it took Ambrose to open Augustine's eyes. Despite all the piety of Epworth Rectory, John Wesley needed a dose of Moravian fervor to light the fire in his heart. Faithful Christian parents are a blessing, but I suspect that for most of us who keep the faith, a crucial role has been played by someone outside the family, someone whose love and wisdom are an unexpected gift.

I was deeply honored to go back to Saint John's yesterday to preach at Mrs. Truax's funeral. She had retired from teaching just a year ago at 93, when one fall too many left her confined to a chair. They were standing in the aisles, dozens upon dozens of her students, grandfathers and grandmothers, teary-eyed young men together with the little girls on the front row who sang so sweetly for her one last time. She taught for fifty-four years, a record probably not soon to be

2 https://livingchurch.org/covenant/problem-with-sunday-school/

surpassed in these days of distraction and volunteer burnout.

I offered the Eucharist today for the repose of her soul, with a prayer for those who continue in her work. Next week, a new teacher or two will start in the Sunday School at my parish, probably in yours as well. He or she might just be the next Mrs. Truax, you know, with God's help, a bit more support and encouragement, and a deeper sense of just how crucial this work really is.

TWENTY-SEVEN

Risky Investments Are the Business of the Kingdom

John Mason Lock

In Psalm 1, we hear of the righteous person, who is a like a "tree plant-ed by streams of living water." The other qualities of the righteous per-son described in the Psalm are arguably more concrete — he does not sit in the seat of the scornful or stand in the way of sinners; he medi-tates on the law of the Lord day and night — so what exactly does it mean to be planted?

As Americans, we are hardly the experts at this. We've long been known for our wanderlust and desire to get away and start a new life. Clergy today are not immune from the impulse to move. As of a few years ago, the average length of tenure for Episcopal clergy was five years. Dean Leander Harding frequently said in his pastoral theology classes that at five years you are still an outsider. If these averages are accurate, it means that most clergy fight through the long period of being an outsider, only to sacrifice it all and move on to the next call.

Since the beginning of the COVID pandemic, we are witnessing a new phenomenon among clergy. They are not just quickly moving from one church to another; they are leaving the ministry altogether. It is the manifestation in the church of a wider trend now called the "great resignation." In August there was a rather public example of this when Alexander Lang, who was the head pastor of a relatively large Presbyterian church outside of Chicago, announced his resignation and departure from the ministry. He wrote[1] about the reasons for this decision on his blog, and the post became a viral moment on social media, especially among clergy who either identified with his bleak assessment of the ministry or condemned him for his lack of tenacity.

In the post, Pastor Lang explains his reasons for leaving the church. He cites things like the burden of carrying other people's secrets, their failures and sins, knowing things that few, if anyone else, knows. He also does not like an overwhelmingly broad job description of the ministry: public speaker, counselor, manager, among others. No person is ever going to be superior in all these fields, but most churches do not understand this. They are looking for Jesus himself, and instead they just get one more sinner.

In the post, Lang also draws back the curtain to reveal the reality that pastor have 1,000 bosses. You answer not only to the church hierarchy and to the vestry or the board. In fact, everyone has a say about

---

1   https://www.restorativefaith.org/post/departure-why-i-left-the-church

your "performance," and they are likely to tell you either directly to your face or indirectly through the rumor mill. Lang also understandably bemoans the many losses pastors endure. This would be a hardship even if it were only for the beloved parishioners you see through sickness, death, and burial. In addition to these losses, there are those who leave the church for any number of reasons. Some move away, but the hardest are those who leave with little or no explanation or warning. In this polarized political environment, people leave because they think you are either too liberal or too conservative, too vocal or too silent about political issues, and it's hard not to internalize all this and think, *Is there something wrong with me?*

Of course what Pastor Lang says is all too true. Even the most sanguine of veteran pastors would have to admit that Lang has not written anything false. The families of pastors could give their testimony to these truths because they often carry their own burdens from the ministry, with few of the "perks." Obviously, Lang highlights the shadow side of the ministry. He does not talk about the tremendous privilege it is to walk with people in the intimate moments of their lives. He does not mention the amazing gift it is to give voice to the grace of God in declaring forgiveness and announcing the goodwill of our Father toward all people. Lang does not talk about how the members of a church put a staggering depth of trust in you as pastor and offer respect for you and the office that is often little deserved or appreciated.

To me the most telling part of Lang's post comes at the end, when he talks about his future plans. He writes, "As for what I plan to do next, I believe one of the most important ways we encounter God's unconditional love is through our relationships with others. I am going to be investing all of my energy into a business that helps people find and form those relationships so they can experience God's love in their lives."

I don't want to vilify Lang or even to say that he has made an immoral choice. He may very well be listening to and obeying God's calling, but I will say that from all appearances it looks like he is running away. I wish I could remind Lang that the place where Christian relationships are formed, where God's unconditional love can be encountered, is supposed to be in the church. The "business" that helps people find and form those relationships so that they can experience God's love in their lives is the local congregation. Lang is leaving the institutional church to start a business that has as its mission doing exactly what the church is designed to do and can do by the grace of God.

For Lang and many other pastors, there is always the tempting allurement of a perfect church that exists somewhere away from the difficulties of the local congregation. Such an ideal congregation, of course, is a figment of the imagination. For a pastor, there is no escape from the challenges Lang describes. These challenges and heartaches are what it means for pastors in particular to take up their cross and follow the Lord.

We might call these sacrifices and hardships the cruciform shape of the ministry. Do not misunderstand me: I am not saying that clergy should become martyrs and just suffer for suffering's sake. I'm also not saying that there are not exceptional cases of clergy abuse in which congregations have done real and lasting harm to a pastor, although frankly the abuse in the vast majority of cases is going in the other direction. I'm talking about the ordinary arc of ministry. Like so many pursuits in life, it can be a grind, but as a Christian vocation it can also be a means of taking up the cross and following the Lord.

For us pastors, a flight away from our calling in the church would only take us from where Christ would have us to be. The church is the place where the sacraments are administered, grace and forgiveness are preached in Jesus' name, people are loved and love each other through good times and bad. It's a cliché that the local congregation is a Christian family, but it is true. We did not pick each other, but Christ has picked us and this is the place where the unconditional love of God meets us, and we learn to love like God loves.

Lang's instinct to fly away is not seen just in pastors. Because to a certain extent we all have illusions of escape. This is frequently evident in marriage, with husbands and wives. They imagine a perfect partner, an ideal marriage, and they think that they can find it out there with someone who is not their spouse. Because, like in the church, there will always be disappointments, points of disjunction, disagreement, and disharmony between a husband and wife. This is the proverbial problem of the grass being greener on the other side.

Most of the time we are just trading one set of known problems for a different set of unknown problems. Of course there are cases of infidelity, abuse, or abandonment, when the marriage is irreparably broken, but in the course of the ordinary Christian marriage, there will be points of discontent and disagreement and even extended seasons when one wonders is this the right fit for me. All married people need to realize is that there is no perfect spouse out there for you. Imagine a post by Pastor Lang's saying he is leaving his marriage to pursue a Christian romance of devotion, loyalty, and selfless love. It sounds absurd because it is. But we flirt with such absurdity in our illusions of escape.

To state the case as simply as possible: Everyone from time to time feels trapped by the confines of life, and the truth is that there is no flight away to some place where you will not sometimes feel trapped or discontent. For Christians, it is the imperfect places and things that are actually the center of where God is working by his grace. God takes imperfect people, imperfect husbands and wives, imperfect churches, and by his mercy and grace he uses them for his purposes.

Consider the faithful priests, pastors, and youth ministers in your life. The ones who have the strongest effect are the ones who did not run away. They didn't try to escape. They did not leave the ministry to form a new business that would do the work of the church, only better. They settled in for the long, slow work of planting seeds, watering faithfully, reaping only as the Lord gave increase. This long, slow, patient work is the inner meaning of the parable of the talents (Matt. 25:14-30). In the kingdom of God, there are those who try to bet "safe." To do so means not to risk anything but to keep all to one's self. This is the servant who takes the talent — a unit of currency in the ancient world — and buries it.

On the other hand, you have the servants who put the talents to good use. There is risk, even catastrophic risk. You could lose some or all of the principal. There could be an accident and you could lose it all. The bank could fail, the investment collapse. To put it in the terms of the ministry: if you accept this calling to be a pastor, you could get hurt and have your heart broken. This is always risk in loving another human being. In the kingdom we are called to take such risks, whatever our calling is.

Our greatest example of this truth is that Christ didn't bury the talent the Father gave him. His whole earthly life was a self-offering, a pouring out. He did not take account of the risk. Born in a stable to a humble young woman, going about doing good, healing the sick, freeing the oppressed, loving all the way to Calvary. For him there was no escape to an ideal Israel. He came to God's people and he loved them to the very end. He made the biggest, most reckless investment by choosing us, the human race, but somehow because he is the Lord, merciful and loving, even in our waywardness and our sin, our luke-warmness and equivocations, he brings increase to his investment, and one day he will present himself together with us, his increase, to the Father.

The Rev. John Mason Lock is the rector of Trinity Episcopal Church in Red Bank, New Jersey. A life-long Episcopalian nurtured in the Diocese of the Rio Grande, he attended the University of Delaware where he majored in English and minored in Jewish Studies. He received his M.Div. from Trinity Episcopal School for Ministry in Ambridge, Pennsylvania, graduating in 2008. He served as curate for five years at All Souls Episcopal Church in Oklahoma City before being called to Trinity Red Bank. He is the proud husband of Bonnie and father of four.

※※※

Made in the USA
Columbia, SC
15 May 2025

57942974R00120